SMALL IN A BIG OCEAN

SAM PRICE

Small Boat in a Big Ocean

Sam Price © 2024

ISBN: 978-1-83663-575-8

All rights reserved. No portion of this book may be reproduced, copied, distributed or adapted in any way, with the exception of certain activities permitted by applicable copyright laws, such as brief quotations in the context of a review or academic work. For permission to publish, distribute or otherwise reproduce this work, please contact the author at samprice0511@outlook.com

A Small Boat in a Big Ocean, dedicated and donated to Royal Manchester Children's Hospital's oncology and bone marrow wards. By Sam "Pampa" Price.

90% of all royalties will be donated to the Cancer and Oncology Department at Royal Manchester Children's Hospital, supported by Manchester Foundation Trust Charity. Remaining 10% of royalties to be held in trust, supporting future treatments for Sorrelle.

Small boat in a big ocean is supporting Manchester Foundation Trust Charity, Reg no 1049274

FOREWORD

The journal you are about to read tells the story of a brave little girl called Sorrelle, her remarkable mother, a supportive family, and this old grandpa's attempt to capture in words the journey of a child battling cancer. Writing this journal became my therapy and my means of coping every day.

I didn't want to meet the new "ward family" because it sadly meant only one thing. But that family helped keep us sane, and gave us all a sense of belonging and the strength to carry on. To this day, I think of that family as fondly as I do my own.

The idea of the journal evolved after spending time with this new family and walking along the quiet nighttime corridors interrupted only by a nurse's smile, another parent's nod, equipment alarms and, yes, a child crying. I began to ponder the days and months ahead. Would Sorrelle survive this? Indeed, would we all survive this, as a family? As the hours became days, it became important to me to do something that would not only help my family but in some small way help families who come to find themselves enduring this unknown and heartbreaking journey. So, on 23rd August 2015 – that I might cast some light on the shadow of this insane situation – the journal began.

My role was simple. I cast myself as the jester, to allow Sorrelle to smile as much as possible and at the same time give my daughter respite from the horrors in front of her, as well as hide my own fears and despair.

If you are a family reading this journal, I can only offer you my sincere thoughts and my heartfelt wish that your journey becomes bearable and that one day you hear your child ring the 'end of treatment' bell. I can promise you that no sound since has had more meaning to me and my family.

That first evening in the hospital, I found myself in the family room, where I met a mum taking a minute to get a drink. She told me about 'the bell' – something I'd never heard of, but why would I? I sat and sobbed at the symbolism of this bell as she told me about children who had finished their treatment, punctuated by the sounding of the bell. And of a mother who rang the bell at the end of treatment on behalf of her child, for a quite different and poignant reason. I felt a little ashamed I hadn't heard of this bell, even if my granddaughter had not been on the ward. Shame on me.

It's impossible to convey how as a family this journey affects you, and it would be foolish not to recognise that this awful disease claims far too many young souls. It's also important to understand that laughter is still possible, that hope must always prevail, that surviving the day gives us the reward of the next.

On one occasion, when waiting for the lift to reach my floor, I saw a teenage girl talking to her mum about what she might like for lunch. Smiles were exchanged, as a younger boy with an IV stand attached to his arm burst into the area with a broad grin, chuckling "What about me?" It was obvious these two young patients had become friends, and what struck me was not the IV stand nor the hair loss but the laughter and smiles. I realised at that point that it is possible to smile. It's a picture I carry with me as a constant reminder that in any circumstances we do have the ability to smile and, moreover, that this lesson is often shown to us by children.

This introduction also allows me to thank a few people involved in this story and in placing it in the public domain.

To Professor Wynn and the remarkably talented medical team who tirelessly fought the cancer, constantly looking for a small adjustment here and a tweak there to enable Sorrelle to fight on – there are no words to adequately convey the depth of feeling we as a family have towards you all.

To Jackie, and many more nurses too numerous to list, who dispensed care, understanding and love to the children and families occupying the ward (you know who you are). To the back-room scientists and blood specialists rarely seen but who provide the diligence and skill needed to support courses of treatment. To the technicians operating the equipment, helping to give vital information. To the cleaners, who are very often the first faces you see on waking after a short respite, for their understanding and warm smiles.

To an anonymous young lady in the London area who gave my granddaughter the chance of life by selflessly donating her bone marrow, not just once but twice – there are simply no words that come close to express our thanks.

To Yasmin Yarwood, of Meticulous Proofreading, who took the journal ramblings of a very emotional grandpa and turned them into a journey to inspire hope.

To Jacqui Peckett, whose artistry could depict this journey with one simple moving picture.

To my amazing little brother Dan who was always there for me personally and helped me keep on going when the days were dark, I miss him terribly and always will.

To our army of family and friends who were always there and able to understand situations when we just could not talk any more.

And two final thank yous. To my daughter Gemma, who showed me the meaning of courage and love. There is no love deeper than that of a mother towards her child. I watched my little girl care for her little girl. I watched my little girl fight for her little girl. I watched my little girl become a ward mother and confidante. I watched my little girl become the remarkable woman she is.

Finally, to Sorrelle. As you read this, Sorrelle, know that you are my inspiration. At such a tender age, you became my hero. You have an incredibly special name that came from my previous hero. You helped me more than you will ever realise, and the impact you have had on your family is indescribable. You are destined for a future all your own. Know as you grow and explore this wonderful thing called life that you will always have with you your "Pampa".

2015

AUGUST 2015

22nd August

Last weekend was just a normal weekend, our granddaughter stayed overnight. As she sat on our bed I tried to coax her into eating a little breakfast, she seemed a little off colour and not as smiley as usual…

Taking her home to my daughter I mentioned Sorrelle seemed a little out of sorts. Later that day my daughter notices a little bruise and with a mother's instinct takes her to the local hospital.

Tonight I got "**that**" call… "Dad, they think it's **LEUKEMIA!**"

23rd August

It's now 2am, we are at Manchester Childrens Hospital gathered around Sorrelle's cot. Professor Wynn enters and he confirms the diagnosis. Our hearts sank and we all began to wonder what this means concluding privately in our own thoughts only one thing!

And so the journey begins…

25th August

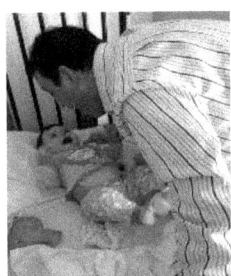

Caption: Yes, Grandpa, you've got the funniest face I've ever seen!

Good evening, all. A little update from Grandpa. I spent a lovely evening with my brave little granddaughter last night. She slept very well and from 4am was asleep in my arms until 8:45am. She is doing really well. The medical team are really happy with her progress, and delighted in the way she is taking the treatment in her stride (while we're all worrying ourselves crazy). It comes as no surprise to us that the nurses are fighting over her!

Just a few days into her chemotherapy and already she is on her way to that first goal of remission! All the tests so far show great signs. I hope you've seen Gemma's information on the JustGiving page for Ward 84. Please do take a look, and if you are able to contribute in Sorrelle's name, that would be wonderful. Keep praying, supporting, hoping, believing – we can all watch Sorrelle beat this.

Grandpa

SEPTEMBER 2015

6th September 2015

Good evening, everyone. Well, today's visit, as you can see, was yet another opportunity for Sorrelle to confound us with her bravery! I can assure you she is smiling – and eating her own body weight in white chocolate buttons and Wotsits! We had a wander around the ward in her walker and then she entertained the next group of visitors! In medical terms, the good news is there is nothing to report, other than one of her doctors informing us that she is just about the easiest patient she's ever had! I think we can all take that as a very good sign :) Sorrelle seems to be tolerating the treatment so well they've decided she doesn't need the anti-sickness drug, so that's one less drug going in her.

Do continue to ask questions and use the group for support. And keep visiting the JustGiving page, where you can see updates on how well the Ward 84 money being raised in Sorrelle's name is doing.

Grandpa

7th September 2015

Caption: Look, Mummy, we have tried crawling out – it didn't work. I think they would notice us trying to row a bath outta here! Put the map away!

Good evening, all. Well, I've just got home from seeing Sorrelle. Time to give you another update and share a couple of pictures with you.

We are now on the 7th day of chemotherapy and there are still no side effects, which I have to say is both fantastic and bemusing. The nurses would certainly have expected some reaction by now, but so far, no aches in her joints, no blisters in her mouth, no nausea and no hair loss. Now, this doesn't mean she's guaranteed no side effects, but it does seem that they will be minimal. We will have to wait and see about her hair.

It is probably a good idea if I let you know the important numbers, so to speak. We need white cells to be low – anything under 10 is great. To put this into context, Sorrelle's were 150 when she was admitted. They're currently 3.7! GREAT! Second, her red blood cells need to stay above 80. When they drop below that, the doctors simply give her more for that all-important energy :) They're 99 at the moment, so that's GREAT, too. Third, her platelets – another fluid that gives us the energy we need – need to stay over 20. If they go under that, they just top her up :) Hers are 77. GREAT. The last two things are her immune system – this takes a bit of a battering, so during treatment Sorrelle is topped up with antibiotics when needed – and her temperature, which needs to stay around 36/37, which it is :)

A chunk to take in, I know, but the important thing is these numbers are really good and show great signs of her moving towards remission! We were told today they do expect Sorrelle to get to remission in the next three weeks and then she could come home! So let's keep everything crossed! We all know we're dealing with something nasty, but honestly the signs are really good.

So, now on to the little lady herself… She's eaten up a storm and had a great bath (which was needed after the choc pudding – pictures to follow!). And I also have the next caption picture to keep you all in good spirits. Finally, can I say, as Gem's dad, how humbled I am by all your support for Gem and Dean. Seeing them each day, I can promise you that the messages, donations and good wishes do make a huge difference. So please accept my heartfelt thanks.

More updates to follow, but for now here's the picture. Enjoy!

8th September 2015

Caption: See, Mummy, I told you they would notice a bath being rowed down the ward! Now they've captured me! Any more bright ideas, Mummy?

By all means think up your own captions, folks 😊 Another tomorrow.

Grandpa

9th September 2015

Good evening, everyone.

Sorrelle, you will all be delighted to know, continues to eat like crazy. She was weighed today and has gained weight, which is always good news, given her treatment. Today's numbers are good, and the doctors and staff seem to be really happy with her. We asked again today about hair loss. Those curls may still leave us in the next week or so, but we will keep you posted about that.

Other news today is insomnia. You may notice the little munchkin's eyes look a little tired – you should see Gemma's! She had a broken night last night and she struggled to sleep today. However, the good news is she officially zonked out around an hour ago. We think she will have a really good sleep tonight. All in all, another good day, all things considered :)

Enjoy the pictures and watch out for the next caption picture :) You will see a theme developing ha ha!

Take care, all.

Grandpa

10th September 2015

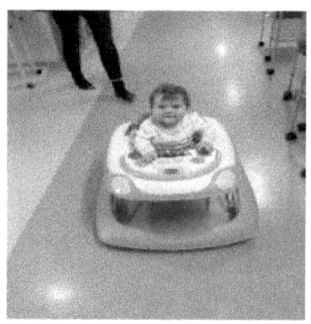

Caption: Mummy hasn't got the hang of this, so I've left her, jumped in my convertible, and I'm off! FREEDOM!

Good afternoon, everyone. So, today's update. 8:30am Coco Pops – and that was it! Onto nil by mouth as Sorrelle had the LP and marrow checks today. So, off she went for a little sleep in theatre. She's totally fine and has come round and is very hungry! See pictures!

The LP is to protect her spine and brain. This is always done as a precaution, so please don't worry. The bone marrow test was a bit of a surprise because there's another in two weeks. Our thinking is that they have been that pleased with Munchie, they may want to test early for remission! We will know the results towards the end of tomorrow, which we will, of course, share with you all.

So, from this morning until 2:30pm, Sorrelle was hungry and a little restless, but since coming round, she has devoured meatballs and mash in a red wine onion gravy, two Milkybar yogurts, handfuls of Wotsits and lots to drink. As you can imagine, she's a little happier now :) Hopefully, she will have a nice, chilled evening and get some much-earned sleep, In the meantime, just so you know, Grandpa has insisted Mummy eats – and she has! Yippee! All in all, another OK day, folks. There will, of course, be a caption picture for you to enjoy. Do, please, let's try and turn Facebook gold for September to raise awareness of child cancer.

Thanks, all.

Grandpa

11th September 2015

Caption: You play chopsticks if you like, Nursey, I'm looking for the door release codes :)

Good afternoon, everyone. Time for your daily Sorrelle update. On my arrival today, I was greeted by the usual smiles and happy face. Her numbers today are OK. White blood cells nice and low (still in single figures), which is where we want them. Her platelets and haemoglobin have dropped a little, but the important word there is LITTLE. No top-ups needed yet and it looks to me as though they're stabilising nicely. Her immune system is low, but aside from crawling around the floor and sticking her hands everywhere, she's staying pretty clean! Seriously, though, she's in a very safe environment, so no concerns about her immune system really.

She had a hearty breakfast but not too much at lunchtime, but she isn't turning away food – by that, I mean Wotsits of course! And white chocolate buttons. I think the Milkybar kid has competition :)

Hope you enjoy today's pictures. Again, if there is anything specific you would like to know, please do ask. Keep all the comments coming from these feeds. Gemma and Dean find them really comforting. Not too much more to report really. Keep asking friends to support Ward 84 and keep turning those profile pictures gold to raise awareness.

One final point – you won't want to miss today's bonus caption picture. Trust me, it's amazing!

Caption: So I was taking out the light fuses ready for my escape, when suddenly there was a bang and it went dark. When the lights came back on – new hair style! Hahaha! ☻

C'mon, folks, you think of some. Gotta be some great ones out there ☻

Grandpa

12th September 2015

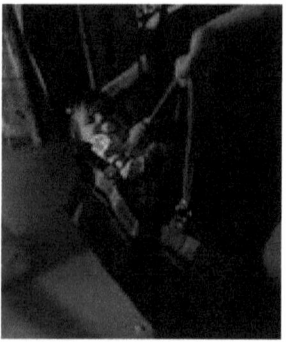

Caption: Finally – a cunning escape plan! This one's in the bag!

A very good afternoon, everyone. A pretty slow news day today. The numbers are all good and still showing signs of stabilising. We are now on day 12 of the chemotherapy, and Munchkin is still taking it in her stride. She does get tired more quickly, and we are giving her different flavours to keep her eating.

Some nice pictures today. She and her friend, Jacob, have taken over the room and are the crowned baby boy and baby girl cuties of the ward :)

Caption picture to follow later! Just wait and see what we have for you all.

Grandpa

13th September 2015

Caption: Of course you can wiggle me all you like, Mummy. I've only had 20 packets of Wotsits and 20 packets of chocolate buttons. What could possibly go wrong! X

Good afternoon, everyone. Well, it's 23 days since Sorrelle was admitted to Ward 84 and nearly three weeks into the chemotherapy. As you can see from today's pictures, our little hero is coping pretty well! Her numbers today are good. She will probably need a top-up of blood and platelets in the next couple of days, but that's perfectly normal. The steroids are giving her insomnia, so the team are going to give her that medication a tiny bit earlier, just to help her try and get through the night with unbroken sleep. Think Mummy could do with some too! The little munchkin had Grandpa's homemade salmon burgers this morning with breakfast – and white choc buttons and Wotsits :)

I want to send a big shout-out to my cousin, Julian, who, despite his own health problems, today completed a 100 km bike ride to raise money for the Christie Hospital – and did so proudly displaying Sorrelle's name :) Thanks, Jules, and to everyone out there who, in so many different ways, is supporting Sorrelle, Gemma and Dean. It truly does mean everything.

As always, the caption picture to follow, so enjoy!

Grandpa

14th September 2015

Caption: You know what, Grandpa? Sometimes cute doesn't need a caption! X

Hi, all. Time for our daily update. Almost three weeks into the chemotherapy and it's starting to catch up a little, although last night Sorrelle got a really good night's sleep and, as you can see, woke up in a great mood :) She had a little breakfast but not much lunch and so she's drinking some milk with the concentrated elements she needs. She's also gone onto anti-nausea medication to help with her eating. She's just polished off some chicken and chips, so I'm sure she'll get back the weight she's lost. Her blood levels climbed on their own today, which is great. She'll probably have platelets on Thursday, judging by the numbers. Her immune system is pretty low, but that's only important if she catches a bug – which she hasn't :)

That's your lot for today, apart from our caption picture. Today's is one to make you go aah.

15th September 2015

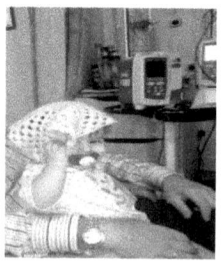

Caption: Naomi Campbell had to start somewhere too! ☺

Good afternoon, all. Blood top-up today, so hopefully a little colour back and more energy too. As for eating, she managed some breakfast, and some macaroni cheese for lunch, with a couple of bottles of milk supplement, so all in all not too bad. She's had some medication to help the toilet situation, which has made her feel a little more comfortable. As for her latest eating craze ... wait for it ... grapes! But not just any old grapes ... grapes that have been peeled by, yep, you guessed it, Grandpa! I've spent much of the afternoon covered in grape juice, carefully removing the skin, so our little princess can feast! Hahaha.

As you can see, the smiles are still there. These photos were taken a couple of hours ago. She also had a visit from the nutritionist, who is happy with things and will monitor her weight and assist when needed. Probably platelets in the next couple of days. You'll have noticed I said she had a blood top-up today. This is because it dipped a little after climbing on its own. That may be why yesterday was a bit of a down day. But listen, folks, she's taking this medication like a champ. She even tries to be happy when she's a bit down! A little hero for sure.

Well, I hope you enjoy the pictures. As always, a caption one to follow.

Grandpa

16th September 2015

Caption: Hang on, Grandpa, I got my looks from where?! :) (My daughters, Sorrelle's mum on the right)

Good evening, everyone. Time for your daily update. Bit of a down day, to be honest. The steroids and chemotherapy fighting each other means that Munchkin's caught in the middle. And despite being so very tired, she's finding it hard to sleep. Last night she didn't sleep too well. Added to which, her platelets are low and she'll need more in the morning. She did, however, have a great breakfast and is drinking the milk supplement, so we reckon her weight should be stable. Her other numbers are OK and her temperature's good. Think today is simply a build-up of the treatment, along with the low platelets. I'm sure she'll be back to her bouncy self in no time.

I've had a word with her, and we've decided on a very special caption for tonight. You'll love it. Trust me!

Grandpa

17th September 2015

Caption: Tell me you've never had a morning like this and I won't believe you :) x

Good afternoon, everyone. Time for Grandpa's update. Better news today and a few more smiles than yesterday. Our little hero is still quite tired but had a decent breakfast and then feasted on roast chicken from Grandpa and more chicken and tuna pasta from Grandma, with lots of milk to wash it down.

As for the numbers today, platelets stayed steady, surprisingly, so looks like no top-up until maybe Saturday. Temp is good, white cells still lovely and low, and immune system actually went up a little. We have the nutritionist here tomorrow for a weigh-in – that's Sorrelle, not the nutritionist! Again, the nurses will give her steroids a little early to try and help her catch up on sleep. Nine more days of the intensive chemotherapy and then we find out how that marrow is doing, so keeping everything crossed.

All in all, better spirits today, folks. We know the journey will have its ups and downs. It just seems that because Sorrelle has coped so well, our downs are more severe, but I need to reassure you that these downs are actually pretty good, given the treatment.

So, try not to worry and enjoy today's smiley pictures. As always, a caption picture to follow.

Grandpa

18th September 2015

Caption: Please notice the badge. If it was good enough for my great-grandpa, then it's good enough for me :) xx

Good afternoon, everyone. Time once again for Grandpa's update. So, here we are, four weeks after diagnosis and three weeks into treatment. As you can see, our brave little girl has retained her ability to smile, soldier on and take whatever they throw at her. Kinda makes you think what's wrong with us! I don't think I'll be complaining about man flu again! Haha.

Today's numbers are pretty good – white cell count very low, but platelets have actually risen! Red blood nice and stable, along with a low but stable immune system. Today is a better day. Breakfast was OK and a lunch of meatballs and homemade tuna pasta filled the spot. As I told you all yesterday, today was a weigh-in. Drum roll, please ... her weight has increased! This is very good news.

Not much more to say about today. As a little aside, I'm delighted to say the JustGiving page hit £600 for Ward 84! Keep goin', folks. Do please keep trying if you're having difficulty with the site. It will work – honestly. I will reshare the link.

Finally, I want to thank you for your comments to these updates and the caption pictures. It really is very warming and gives great support to Gem and Dean.

Grandpa

19th September 2015

Caption: Mirror, mirror, on the wall… Oh, forget it, we know the answer

Good afternoon, all. Time for the daily update. Another pretty good day today. Platelets have again risen on their own, which is great, but do remember there's been a day's break in chemotherapy, so there's nothing killing the platelets – this is normal. Still good that the bone marrow is making them, though. Red count has only dropped a little, and white cells remain nice and low at .09 :) Temperature fine and indicates no bugs. Given she has a very low immune system, it's good she's staying healthy. One less thing to worry about.

Breakfast was OK today, and lots of milk supplement, so I am sure the weight Sorrelle has gained can be maintained. Didn't have much for lunch, but she spent a chunk of the afternoon sat on Grandpa's knee scoffing chicken, sausage and carrot sticks :) She also seems a little happier and more settled today. More medication now and hopefully another good night's sleep.

Grandpa

20th September 2015

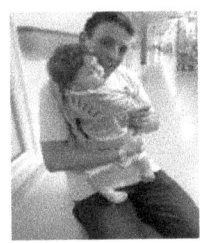

Caption: Following Manchester City's dismal display to the media yesterday – here's their new striker! hehe xx

Good afternoon once again, family and friends. Today's update:

Breakfast: Eaten, Lunch: Eaten, Snacks: A fair few, Milk: 2 bottles !

Numbers: Platelets risen again. Red count high and stable. Temperature spot on!

Generally, as adorable as ever

Good day today, folks. Our little hero seems back to her old self. I think a day or so between chemotherapy clearly makes a big difference. In fact, as we speak, she is filling her gorgeous little face with tuna pasta. Lots of smiles today and much more chilled. Another day nearer to beating the c—p out of this thing!

Oh, and the caption is good fun, too. Well, at least for one half of Manchester, following Mummy's shopping trip.

Enjoy the pictures, folks. See you tomorrow.

Grandpa

21ˢᵗ September 2015

Caption: So, you're telling me, when I'm 24 and crazy, I'll be able to pull that face, too, Mummy! :) xx

Good evening, everyone. I've just got home from visiting our little hero. So, today's news. Well, apart from screaming the place down when Grandpa dared give her to Mummy while he went to get a coffee, she's been a little darlin' :) Has eaten well. For breakfast, tuna pasta! For lunch, tuna pasta! For dinner, yep, you guessed it! And lots of milk supplement. She will be wanting gondolas and opera next! As for the numbers, red blood and platelets are rising and stable. White cells still nice and low, and immune system has risen a little, but still a long way to go with this. We found out today it's unlikely Sorrelle will be out before her birthday at the end of October, but to be honest, as long as she's in the best place to treat her, then it'll be fine. The reality is she does everything in here that she would do at home, so she isn't missing out on anything. Her temp is a tiny bit high, getting a cold we think, but not high enough to need any medication, so all in all a pretty good day. She smiled a bit more today and fell asleep around 8:15pm while Grandpa was stroking her toes :)

Grandpa

22nd September 2015

Caption: Hell, yes, I'm grumpy. You go through all this treatment and other people try and muscle in!

Good evening, everyone. Time for our daily dose of hero worship. So, numbers today. Platelets rising big time on their own! This is great. Red count fell a little, but hey we can't have everything. Immune system's stable, which is great. Temp is fluctuating a little but staying under 38, so nothing to be concerned about. As for food, well, it's been a tuna pasta day again! Oh, I tell a lie – she had salmon pasta for lunch! Wow, this girl can vary her menu :) Other than that, as you can see, more smiles from our little munchkin. Apart from the caption picture coming up, there's a little grump peeking through, but you'll see why…

Another pretty good day. As I write this, the gorgeous Sorrelle is cosy and fast asleep :)

Night, all.

Grandpa

23rd September 2015

Caption: Know your Disney? Which one's Maleficent, and which one's Aurora?! I'll let you decide…

Good afternoon, everyone. Hang on, let me do that again. A VERY good afternoon, everyone :) Why? I hear you ask. Well, soon as the drum roll's subsided, I'll tell ya :) OK, here we go, today's numbers… Platelets haven't just risen, they've gone through the roof! Up from 87 to nearly 200! Red count over 100! Immune system up from 0.02 to 0.28! And white cells still in single figures. Now, I know she's had a couple of days without chemotherapy and so her body's had a chance to recover, but really, folks, it's great news Munchkin's body's reacting so well! Great sign. Her temp's hovering around 37. Bit of a cold still, but that's being monitored. As for eating, three words really – like a pig! Hahaha.

The next bone marrow test is next Wednesday and then we will find out about remission and treatment plans. Only other thing to report is those curly locks are starting to thin a little. We knew it was coming, but I reckon our little hero will be fashioning a new trend of headbands soon.

A good day, people. Enjoy the pictures. Great caption picture tomorrow. Trust me!

Grandpa

24th September 2015

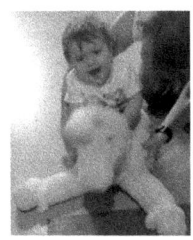

Caption: I know what you're thinking ... he can't take the weight, so it was either ride him or eat him! Hahaha x

Good afternoon, all. Time for today's update. Not too much change today other than to say the numbers have dropped a little, but this is due to a dose of chemotherapy last night. Still very good, though. It's kinda like our baseline is now higher, even with treatment. Docs and nurses still really happy with her, and she's still smiling her way through 😊 As for eating, well, look at the pictures and I reckon you'll have the answer! A real little chunk – and it's not just the steroids. Weigh-in day tomorrow – my money's on needing bigger scales! The caption picture will sum it up beautifully :)

Well, enjoy the pictures, everyone, and once again thank you for all the comments you put on them. It's great for Gem and Dean to read 😊

Grandpa

25th September 2015

Caption: Bye bye, prison bars!

Good evening, all. Very appropriate pictures tonight – just mummy and daughter :) So, today's news! Well, if I met the professor of happy from the university of happy, he still wouldn't be as happy as we are today! So, what's the news? Get on with it, Grandpa! Haha, OK then. Well, numbers today – no, forget them, let's get straight to the headlines… SHE'S COMING HOME! Yep, you read that correctly! After five weeks of treatment, the doctors are that happy with our little hero they're giving her some freedom! Tomorrow night she'll go home, maybe for a night and a day. Not long to us but a massive stepping stone. This only happens if the medics are happy with how the child responds to treatment.

Let's all enjoy the news and the pictures. Laugh, cheer, cry, party, clap. Have a great evening, folks.

A very happy Grandpa :) x

26th September 2015

Hey, Cuz, I'll hide under the duvet and stay. They'll never notice and then ...
PARTY!

Good evening, all. Good news and not-so-good news tonight. Let's get the bad news out of the way first – Sorrelle wasn't allowed out for the night after all ☹ Gem, as you can imagine, is really upset. Bit of a mix-up in communication between the consultant and the professor. Guess we just have to accept decisions are made in Sorrelle's best interest, even though it wasn't until the eleventh hour when Gem was told.

On a brighter note, our little hero had a good day, with visits from Uncle Dave, Auntie Anna, Uncle Mark, Auntie Rachel and cousin Arthur :) Her numbers were really good today, which makes the decision more frustrating, but we can't forget we are dealing with infant ALL – which means the regime is much stricter.

Grandpa

27th September 2015

Caption: Tell them I have a very special set of skills. I WILL find them. And I WILL eat them 😊

Good afternoon, everyone. Time for our daily update. Well, let's just call yesterday a very tough, frustrating day, losing that freedom at the last minute. But today we are better, brighter and refreshed! Numbers first. All very good – red count high, platelets through the roof, white cells low, immune system low but stable. Better news is that our little hero finally had a much better night's sleep and therefore so did Mummy. Let out onto the grass today in the sunshine, and a day full of smiles :) Can't tell you just how important days like today are.

Moving nearer to the all-important marrow test on Wednesday.

A much happier Grandpa today. Have a good evening and enjoy the picture.

Grandpa

28th September 2015

Caption: Hey, Grandpa, did you hear the news today? They let me go home.

I sure did, Sorrelle. This is what a happy Grandpa looks like! x

A VERY good evening, everyone. So, today's news is pretty low-key really! OK, the truth ... she is free! Amazing news. They are so pleased with Sorrelle – and recognise what an amazing pair of parents she has – they have finally allowed her home, until Wednesday, when she'll return for the bone marrow test. It's a pretty happy day 😊

So today's caption comes with a warning. Those of a nervous disposition may want to have medication on standby! Hahaha. You all realise I do these posts to inform you but also to give comfort to Gem and Dean in my own small way. I made Gem a promise today about the caption picture, despite the fact it will do me no favours. I know she will giggle lots, and so my embarrassment will be well worth it. Enjoy it, folks – it won't be happening again :)

I'd just like to mention some other heroes out there – you happy band of walkers who've given up your time tonight to raise awareness and money for Ward 84 in Sorrelle's name :) As you end your walk, I'd like to thank you all, from my heart. YOU are making a difference to those children out there battling this horrific disease, and the support, love and kindness you have shown to my daughter, Dean and Sorrelle would warm even the coldest of hearts. You are my heroes. Thank you.

Sorrelle's Grandpa

Grandpa x

29th September 2015

Caption: After all the ingenious ways I thought of to escape, you put me in a shopping trolley! :) x

Good afternoon, everyone. Time for another in the daily update series. Now, as you can imagine, Gem and Dean were nervous about our hero being out of hospital – and what to expect. I am sure many of you are wondering how it's been. Well, let me give you the update.

The numbers...

Red count: haven't a clue, Platelets: haven't a clue, White cells: haven't a clue' Temp: 37.3 – perfectly normal, Sleep: 100% better 😊, Eating: better 😊, Smiles: better 😊.

Gemma: the same – eating better, sleeping better and smiling better 😊

Dean: yikes! – Gemma back home. Hehehe!

The pictures tell it all, folks 😊 Now tomorrow, as we know, is a very important day – the bone marrow test. We'll discover if our little hero has got to that stage of remission we're all hoping for. With luck, we'll know the results tomorrow. So, bear with us. Soon as we know, we will let you know.

Back to normal caption picture today, you'll all be delighted to hear. No more Grandpa parading around in straw hats and pink shorts :)

Enjoy the picture and have a good day, everyone.

Grandpa

30th September 2015

Caption: Grandma, this won't work unless you feed it to me 😃xx

Good afternoon, everyone. Well, the latest news is there won't be any news 🙁 When they got to the hospital and took Sorrelle's temperature, it was 38.5. This means she has to have antibiotics for 48 hours before any procedure can be done. Although it's very frustrating this can happen – and we would have expected it at some point – it's frustrating it had to happen today. She's a little warm but otherwise in great shape. They have readmitted her and done the numbers, which all look pretty good. Her immune system has even gone up. So, most importantly, don't worry – our little hero is just fine. By all means be as frustrated as hell, though! Gem and Dean are, but they're also in pretty good spirits as Sorrelle had a couple of lovely days at home. So, it's looking like Friday at the earliest before we know about hope of remission. As always, I'll keep you posted.

Caption, of course, to follow.

Grandpa

OCTOBER 2015

1st October 2015

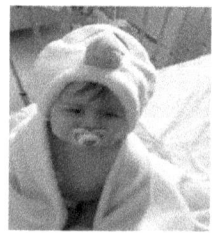

Caption: *That's Cleopatra to you* 😊 x

Good afternoon, everyone. Update time from the world of Sorrelle. Firstly, that dastardly temperature! It's been fluctuating, with a high of 41.5, and is currently around 38.4. It needs to be under 38 for 48 hours before the bone marrow test can be done, so it's likely there's going to be an extended stay in hospital. The antibiotics should take effect over the next 36 hours and steady her temp. As for the eating, not too bad, although if we had a high temp, we probably wouldn't be that peckish.

Most importantly, she is OK, safe and in the right place. And, of course, she had that break at home, which has done her and Mummy and Daddy the world of good. On with the fight. Latest pictures from today and last night so you can see, though sleepy and warm, she's doing OK.

Caption picture I have to say is pretty cute, even though I'm a tad biased :)

Grandpa

2nd October 2015

Caption: This is what true inspiration looks like.

Good afternoon, everyone. Time for the Sorrelle news. She's back on Ward 84 receiving excellent care. Turns out the temperature increases are due to a blood infection, which they have under control. Our little hero is comfortable and she has started to drink a bit more and food is OK. The numbers today are OK. Red count 98, following a bag of blood last night. Platelets are down, at 57, which is normal with an infection and, as we know, these can be boosted when needed. Her immune system is at 1.88, which is an increase – which I know seems odd if she has an infection. It's now likely the bone marrow test won't happen until Wednesday and then it'll be straight into the next round of treatment, so we're looking at another four weeks on Ward 84 before any chance of a break at home. One thing we are all learning is that the next two years are likely to be this very same roller coaster. So, stay strong, everyone. We're in this for the long haul, but what a reward there will be at the end 😊

Oh, and today's caption is a timely reminder to us all that there are some special people out there 😊

Grandpa

3rd October 2015

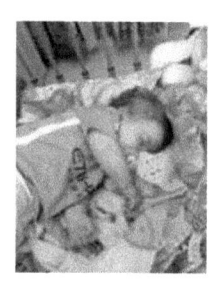

Caption: A 6-1 goal fest today. Of course I'm tired.

Good evening. everyone. Time for your next update. The infection in Sorrelle's blood was a bit of a new one for the nurses. However, the guys in the labs knew of it and have given her the appropriate antibiotics. The numbers for tonight are pretty solid, and, importantly, her temp has stayed normal for over 24 hours, so we're on course to do the bone marrow test on Wednesday and then on to the next stages of treatment. Eating and drinking have been OK, and as you can see from the pictures, that bright, sunny disposition carries right on 😊 Not much else to tell you, folks. If you haven't already seen Wednesday's Bolton News, you might enjoy the read 😊

See you all tomorrow.

Grandpa

4th October 2015

Caption: Don't worry, Daddy, I know you've had a bad day, but I'm here to help. It's Hug a Manchester United Fan Day today 😂

Good evening, everyone. After a week's break, I returned to the hospital tonight, and it seems I was missed – just a little perhaps ☺ Today's numbers are very similar to yesterday's, so nothing to report there. Good news that the temperature has again stayed low, currently at 37.1, which is where it needs to be. As for eating and drinking, well, we have a bit of a challenge there. Our little hero seems to be off it a little. We have a visit from the nutritionist tomorrow to put a plan in place. Other than that, as you can all see, the smiles still light up the ward and help us too ☺

Tonight's caption will be comforting to Daddy ☺

See you all tomorrow.

Grandpa

5th October 2015

Caption: Thought I'd share a photo from my old days, posing in my very own calendar. Or is that colander? 😂

Good afternoon, everyone. Time for the Sorrelle news. The temperature situation continues to remain stable and, so far, Wednesday is still the day for the bone marrow test. The professor called in this morning. Again, very happy with our hero and doesn't seem concerned by the lack of eating and drinking. As he put it, we're surprised she's got this far into treatment without needing tubes, and she is still eating a little bit. The numbers for today seem stable. Not really anything to report, apart from her immune system has improved slightly :)

Not a great night's sleep last night. In fact, no sleep until around 6:30am! So, you can imagine how chilled Gemjar was this morning 😊 Well, that's all for today. An old picture for today's caption, but it's a belter 😊

See you all tomorrow.

Grandpa

6th October 2015

Caption: Yes, that's right, Grandpa, you are now my PA 😁 Now do as you are told and take my calls!

Good afternoon, everyone. Tuesday's news. Well, temperature today has stayed constant and we're still on course for the bone marrow test tomorrow. More antibiotics today to remove the infection from Sorrelle's line. Numbers today – nothing much to report other than a drop in her immune system, but remember this is all normal stuff. You regular readers will be pretty expert at all this soon – though don't take Gem on in a quiz! As for food and drink, well, not much drink really. Pretty sure in a day or two they will help her along with some fluids. As for food, better news there. A jar and a half of her new favourite food at lunchtime – baby food! Yep, the yucky stuff! Hahaha.

Today's pictures show you she is happy and still smiling. For the more eagle-eyed among you, you'll see those curls are thinning. Again, in the grand scheme of things, our little hero is doing real good, and from what I've seen, her side effects are pretty mild.

Well, that's it for today, folks. Will be back again tomorrow.

Grandpa

7th October 2015

Caption: Hey, Grandpa. I kinda like this grandpa/granddaughter quiet time thing.

Good afternoon, everyone. Just a little note to let you all know that today's update will be later this evening. Sorrelle is having the bone marrow test today, so we want to leave it until later to update you all. Our little hero will be going for the procedure in the next half hour, so let's all keep everything crossed 😊

Grandpa

Good evening, everyone. Let's get the waiting out of the way first. Gonna be a delay, I'm afraid. We won't know any results until tomorrow. They were busy doing procedures today and haven't had time to get back to us. So, rest of the news for today… Platelets are increasing on their own, her immune system's rising, red count's good, temperature's normal – so all in all a pretty good day. As for food and drink, a little more today, which is good. You can see from the pictures the little sparkle has returned to her eyes. She's not looking as tired and has had a couple of decent nights' sleep. Not much more to tell you. Tomorrow's the big day, when we get information from under the microscope about how she's responding to treatment. Here's hoping, folks 😊

Grandpa

8th October 2015

GOOD MORNING EVERYONE!

As promised, some news for you. Thought I would use this picture again but change the caption.

Caption: Hey, Grandpa, while we are sat here all quiet, I need to tell you something.

What, Munchkin?

I'm in REMISSION, Grandpa! I'm glad you're sat down. Now stop crying :)

Yes, everyone, you read that correctly. Six weeks into this fight, and our little hero is in remission! Have to say there are some tears flowing here. We know we have a long road of treatment ahead and there will be some poorly days, but this news is amazing. No traces in her bone marrow!

Now we enter the period where we aim to have our little hero cancer-free in two years. We'll know the treatment plan in the next day or two, so watch out for this on the posts. I will post later tonight but for now let's just enjoy that word – and those tears of joy!

REMISSION – REMISSION – REMISSION!

Caption: Mummy and Daddy, my family everywhere in the world, my friends, my nice doctors and nurses – I just want to tell you, this fame and remission lark is pretty tiring. Night night and happy dreams.

Good evening, everyone. Time for the daily update. Oh, did I tell you… REMISSION!

🎂🍦🎂🍦🎂🍦🎂🍦🎉🎉🎉🎉🎉🎉🎉🎉‼‼‼Oh yes, so I did 😊

Today's numbers. Who cares! No seriously, though… Platelets have risen on their own from 84 to 186, which is great. Red count has fallen, so a blood top-up tonight. Her immune system has increased. Temperature is normal. So, all good on the numbers front. Tomorrow, Sorrelle will have her Hickman line taken out as this is where the infections have been. A simple procedure – she will have a sleep for 20 minutes or so and might be a little sore, but she'll be fine. Then, after a few days, they will resite the line to administer the medication. Until then, they will probably put in a cannula.

In tonight's picture you will notice those curls are thinning a fair bit, but so what, I hear you say – and rightly so 😊 She's in remission and that's good enough for us all right now. Those cheeky eyes and the smile are there. Enjoy tonight, folks. I can assure you Sorrelle has a very happy mummy and daddy, who are very much enjoying this important day and are loving all the comments you're sending. Caption picture to follow, to finish the evening perfectly.

Take care, all. So very happy to write today's posts 😊

Grandpa

9th October 2015

Caption: I've said it before and I'll say it again – sometimes cute doesn't need captions.

Good evening, everyone. It's update time. So, first up, today's numbers. White cells low, platelets high, red count high, immune system down a little and temperature normal. Pretty boring stuff, hey. But ee bah gum, as they say up here, boring looks great when underpinned by REMISSION 😊 (We do love saying that hahaha.) So, rest of today's news… Munchie had her Hickman line taken out today. They will put a new one in on Monday and probably start the next round of chemotherapy on Tuesday. After she came round from theatre, she tucked into a sausage roll, chips and gravy and then polished off another half a sausage roll. Drinking better too.

As you can see from the pictures, that smile is still shining brightly and there are a few curls hanging on for dear life, bless 'em. That's about it for today. Will come up with a caption picture for you all to enjoy, maybe back in time a little 😊

Enjoy your evenings, everyone.

Grandpa

10th October 2015

Caption: If I were you, I'd get some sleep too, Grandpa. You're gonna be busy later 😂

Good evening, everyone. Well, the big news today is that there isn't really much news 😊 Because there is no line in, no bloods were taken today and therefore there are no numbers to report. What I can tell you is that her temperature has remained perfect all day and there seems to be some natural colour returning to our little hero. As for food and drink, pretty good this morning, but not too much later. I expect a bit of a bite to eat later.

Grandpa has the night shift tonight, so I'm sure I'll have tales to tell tomorrow. As I post, Sorrelle is sleeping sweetly, presumably to keep Grandpa awake through the night! But hey, like I care – I get to see more of that smile 😊 Gemma and Katie are having a girlie night, and I have my instructions to cook them breakfast in the morning. So, anyone willing to donate a couple of matchsticks for my eyes, then there's a breakfast in it for you here in the morning 😂

Have a good evening, everyone.

Grandpa

11th October 2015

Today's caption is the picture of Sorrelle and Grandpa looking at the other picture you can all see 😂

Caption: Let's keep looking to make sure, Grandpa… But I'm sure that's Mummy on the left and my godmummy on the right. Is it too late to replace them? 😂 xxx

Good afternoon, everyone. Time for today's little hero news. Again, no numbers for you today as we are waiting for blood tests to be done, but the fact they're not concerned about timely tests suggests they're more than happy with our little hero.

So, last night and Grandpa's sleepover … a piece of cake hahaha. She slept from 10:30pm until 7:45am, with one five-minute spell while being medicated :) So, Munchkin, thank you for letting Grandpa sleep 😂 Mummy is very jealous! Then at 10am this morning I cooked breakfast for a rather tired-looking Gemma and Katie, and our little munchkin sat with us and even helped herself to some toast and bacon. She has started to eat a little more and her drinking is getting better too. The cannula has been removed, so no other medication today other than oral antibiotics. Tomorrow the new Hickman line goes in, so a little trip to theatre at some point, then the next round of chemotherapy can be scheduled.

As you can see from the pictures, she continues to smile through this, and those curls are still hanging in there 😊

Enjoy the smiles

Grandpa

12th October 2015

Caption: Time to rest, Daddy, just before I beat the c—p out of this disease! ☺

Good evening, everyone. 51st day today, and we now move into phase two. The first six or seven weeks moved our little hero to remission. Now we begin the long, hard journey to being cancer-free. The two years start here. As I speak, our little hero is having her Hickman line put in so her treatment can start tomorrow. There will be three sets of 10-day highly intensive chemotherapy over the next three months, with time in between for Sorrelle to recover. Difficult days do lie ahead, folks. There will be more side effects and she will be uncomfortable. It's not going to be easy knowing our little hero is struggling, but we have to keep our minds on the prize – a life and a future cancer-free. We will be honest with you and we will continue to send you pictures of that smile.

As for today's numbers, they are actually really good. Today is the start of the new phase, so let's all enjoy tonight's pictures and the smiles. Send positive thoughts over to our hero and indeed to Gem and Dean. You have all been a wonderful support and, as I have said many times, your comments are a real comfort, now more than ever. Keep those comments coming and above all else keep positive and keep smiling. She will beat this, folks, no matter how long the journey.

Grandpa

13th October 2015

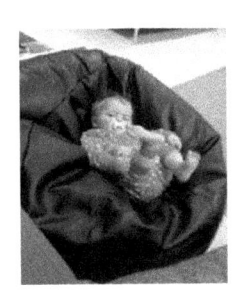

Caption: Ah, good evening, Mr Bond. What have you done with my white cat?!

Good evening, everyone. Time for today's update. Thought we would give you a video today instead of pictures 😊 So, her numbers are very good. Platelets high, red count high, immune system high and temperature normal – simply perfect. Have to say it's probably the last day for a while that the numbers will be so good. First day of intensive chemotherapy starts in around an hour from now. We know it's gonna be tough, but, as I said last night, we have to keep focused on the prize. Our little hero is currently fast asleep, partly because she didn't sleep too well last night. Hopefully she will catch up tonight.

Food and drink have been OK, nothing to shout about. She's lost a tiny bit of weight, but she's still the correct weight for her age, so no massive concerns. That's about it for today, folks.

Grandpa

14th October 2015

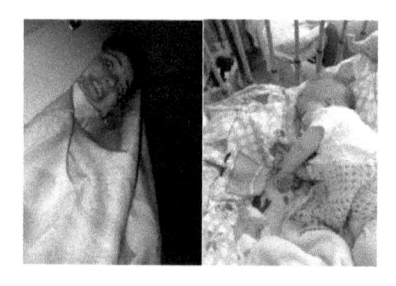

Double picture caption: How is a girl supposed to sleep?

Good evening, everyone. Yep, time for your daily update. Firstly, the numbers. One word – great! Platelets are nice and high – same with the red count – her immune system is really good, and her temperature's normal. Any immune measurement over 0.50 means she's allowed off the ward. It's currently 1.51 😊 We know breaks and fresh air won't be possible in the weeks to come, so we're making the most of this now.

Yesterday was day one of the treatment plan, and today Sorrelle was happy, chirpy and had food and juice. We had a little surprise, in that she had to have a lumbar puncture, so she was nil by mouth again. Frustrating but it's all part of the process. As you can see from the pictures, that gorgeous smile is still there. And she's sporting a cow onesie!

Chemotherapy scheduled for 9pm tonight and day two. So far so good.

Have a good evening, everyone.

Grandpa

15th October 2015

Caption: Hey, Cuz, thinking about you and love you. Looking forward to us getting into mischief together when I come to visit soon 😊

Good evening, everyone. Today's news. Day 2 of the new treatment plan and, as always, our little hero continues to swagger through 😊 Numbers today are still high. However, she has had a couple of high temperatures due to the new chemotherapy. She's on antibiotics just in case, but the doctors do expect these fluctuations in temperature. As for food and drink, Munchie's had a bit, but unless she starts to eat more, it won't be enough to avoid the dreaded tube feeds. Monitoring this as we go, but overall, she's doing so very well with the treatment. Well, that's all for tonight. Grandpa

Grandpa

16th October 2015

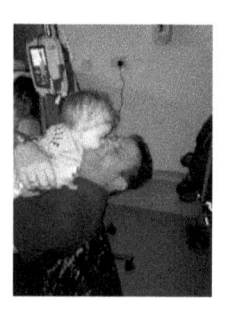

Caption: Blimey, Grandpa, it would've been easier scaling Everest!

Good evening, all. Today's news. Well, last night was a bit of a bumpy ride. Temperature rose a little, and she was a bit sick. This morning was better, and she's eating and drinking plenty. Other good news – there's been an increase in weight and, no, I don't mean me! Immune system has dropped a fair bit, but her temperature today has been good. Red count was low, so, as I post this, our little hero is having a top-up of that lovely red stuff. No, not wine! Hahaha!

Fourth day of 10 on the new treatments and as well as can be expected really. Enjoy the pictures, and I'll see you all tomorrow. Do take a look at the hamper post if you haven't already and let me know if you'd like tickets.

Grandpa

17th October 2015

Caption: What has a girl gotta do? You do cute, you do smiles, you do brave and STILL the bars!

Good evening, everyone. Tonight's update is short, mainly because our little hero has had a pretty good day. Food and drink OK. Numbers are good and consistent. Her immune system has dropped a little but is still high enough to not be a concern. Sorrelle continues to take the medication in her stride and, quite frankly, she has more courage and resolve than I've ever seen. I know I'm biased, but she really is a remarkable little girl. Tonight, Grandpa has a sleepover with the little hero. I'll be sure to get myself plenty of cuddles 😊 Took a lot of persuading to get Mummy to have a relax tonight, and I had to promise to phone her if needed. Sorrelle and I have a deal that she's gonna sleep through, so all should be just fine 😊

Well, not much more to tell you, other than she really is getting used to the new round of medication.

Take care, all.

Grandpa

18th October 2015

Caption: No words, just look

Good evening, everyone. Well, what an amazing day! One word for her numbers – fantastic 😊 The day started with smiles and giggles, then we all had a full Daddy breakfast together (Grandpa breakfast to Munchkin). Apparently, they're famous 😊 Then a late-morning snooze before lunch, and this afternoon a bath! That, our little hero loved to bits. Now this is important, because she has really not liked them since being in hospital, and bathtime was always one of her favourite things. So, today has been a really great day. Gem and Dean had a great night's rest last night and recharged their batteries – Team Sorrelle has had a really good weekend. You can tell from the pictures she's perking up.

The caption picture is amazing. I challenge you to take a good look and not have a lump in your throat :)

Have a great evening, people.

Grandpa 😊

Hey, Grandpa. It's 1am. Here's an interesting concept for you. My chemotherapy just finished, and now I need a 20-minute flush … which takes 60 minutes! Does that mean they should call it a 60-minute flush then?!

YES, Munchkin, they should!

Then that's crazy, Grandpa!

YES, Munchkin, it is!

19th October 2015

Caption: Me and Mummy with piggy. And Peppa too! Hahaha 😄

Good evening, all. News time. Again, a really good day. Good night's sleep and toast for breakfast 😄 As for the rest of the day, not much for lunch or dinner really. Weigh-in day tomorrow, and we're expecting her weight to be OK. Numbers today are lower but still good, as is her temperature.

We had a birthday on the ward and a visit from a rather famous pig, so it was a happy day today. That's about it for today. Keep well, everyone.

Grandpa

20th October 2015

Caption: We could play peekaboo. Or you could just look at me? 😄

Good evening, everyone. There's not much to update as there were no bloods taken and therefore no results. What I can say is that our little hero has had another day of smiles and giggles 😄 Eating was OK today, but there has been a little weight loss and so we will need to continue looking for taste sensations to encourage her. As you can see from the pictures, Munchkin is getting more gorgeous every day 😄

Caption to follow. Have a good evening, everyone.

Grandpa

21st October 2015

Caption: Yes, Daddy, of course you're interesting and, yes, I'm listening.

Evening, everyone. Time for your daily Sorrelle update. Well, we have the numbers today and they are OK – red count and platelets are nice and high and temperature still normal. Her immune system, however, is starting to crash, meaning she's open to infection. The doctors expect her temperature to spike and when it does, they'll be ready with antibiotics. The last day of the first 10-day treatment cycle is on Friday. Following this, her numbers will start to reduce before they recover. This will take approx. three weeks, and once her counts start to improve, then tests will be done to measure the success of the first 10 days. Then, the second 10-day treatment will begin. She is well in herself and smiling as always 😊 So, as before, we enjoy these days and prepare for the rough ones to come.

Enjoy the pictures of our little hero.

Have a good evening, all.

Grandpa

22nd October 2015

Caption: Can't a girl get a little privacy?

Good afternoon, everyone. Time for today's update. Sorrelle's immune system has got lower, so she's confined to the ward. Other numbers have again reduced, but this is what they'd expect – and our little hero is smiling through it 😊 Her temperature has returned to normal, so no real concerns there. To be honest, the biggest challenge at the moment is eating. Drinking, even milk, is pretty good, but her appetite really fluctuates. All part of the roller coaster, but it is a lovely sight when she eats, and we could all do with seeing it again soon. Not saying that she's not eating at all, but it could be better. Worst-case scenario, there's always the dreaded food tube. The good news is, whatever the issues, they have solutions here. Well, that's it once again for another day.

Have a good evening, all, and enjoy the picture.

Grandpa

23rd October 2015

Caption: Yes, I know you've seen it before, but you can never have too much of a good thing.

Good afternoon, everyone. So today's news – immune system officially zero! So, watch out, infection city! Temperature is good and platelets are fine. Will need more blood tomorrow, though, to perk her up. Now the food… Well, Grandpa tried the 'ignore and pinch mine' approach. It worked a little. 3 chips, 2 little pieces of sausage roll, 3 spoons of chocolate mousse, a third of a banana and the odd swig of milk … wait for it … out of the container! Then 20 minutes to clean my trousers. It wasn't a bad mission! There is a but, though. She needs to eat more. They're going to check again on Monday, so we have a stay of execution. We have to keep that habit of eating going. Other than that, as you'd expect, she's still wowing them on the ward. This picture was taken five minutes ago. Well, hey, a girl's gotta rest 😊

Have a good evening, everyone.

Grandpa

24ᵗʰ October 2015

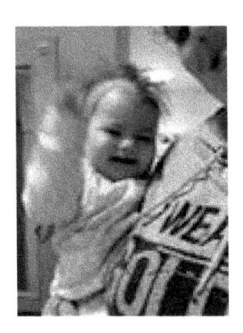

Caption: Bit poorly tonight, but the smile will be back real soon.

Good evening, everyone. Tonight's update's gonna be brief. Sadly, not too many smiles today. Sorrelle has started to get the sores in her mouth and throat that we feared, so eating and drinking has become painful. As a result, they've had to put a tube in to feed her through and to give her medication for the pain. Seems odd her immune system's got better, but at the same time this. We have to remember, folks, that this was coming. It's the time we need to be strong. And let's all try and remember that she is still in remission, and we are beating this. It's simply that there are going to be bad days to get through and this is one of them. So, there is a little girl and her mummy and daddy who could do with lots of comments tonight. Let's help them through what I think is going to be a long night.

Take care, everyone.

Grandpa

25th October 2015

Caption: Mums try new approach to help their children sleep on Ward 84 😂

Good afternoon, everyone. Sorrelle news time. I can imagine after my update yesterday you were all a little concerned, so I thought I would get today's update in nice and early to help any anxiety. Truth is, last night wasn't great. Sorrelle had some sleep but was then sick and pulled out her tube ☹️ Thankfully, they left it out for a while so as not to distress her further. We think the feed was a little too much for her to cope with, but the nurses had to give her something before the nutritionist comes in on Monday (the nutritionist decides the size and frequency of the feeds). Her nappies are getting pretty full, and both of these things confirm mucositis (sores from the mouth downwards, basically). There is still the pain relief, but it's a side effect of the treatment that I'm afraid she has to endure. Our little hero is still just that, and when I visited today I was amazed that after the 24 hours she's had, she still wants to smile 🙂 She has demonstrated more courage during these weeks than I have in my lifetime!

So, this morning, they put the tube back in, and so far, it's still there. If she pulls it out again, then they will feed her differently. It'll involve being hooked up but it'll be a lot less distressing and less invasive. As you can see from the pictures today, Sorrelle is trying hard, bless her. But I have to report that, put simply, things have changed. There's more evidence of side effects, pain, discomfort and upset. This, as you can imagine, will take its toll not only on Sorrelle but on Gemma and Dean too. They are being so strong for Sorrelle, but they are tired. The nights are long, the sleep is short, emotions are high, and so, in my humble opinion, I think they need our help … all three of them! Especially now we have entered this new phase of treatment with all its difficulties. The help I'd suggest is in three key areas:

1. Messages of support and comments – essential

2. Visits – very important

3. Times of visits – carefully planned

I think now that sleep has been much more affected, we need to make sure Gemma and Dean are working together to support each other's rest. Could I suggest that when you know you are free to visit that you message Gemma and Dean just so they can manage times and make sure they have some rest time. I know if we could, we would all be living on the ward together, but this new treatment is having a big impact on Gem and Dean and, in honesty, they need to manage their rest time better. The problem is they don't want to say to people not to come – and we do all need to still visit – but what they don't realise, bless them, is that we won't feel hurt if they say no once in a while. 😊

So, folks, when you comment on this post tonight, please reassure Gem and Dean that we won't feel hurt – and that they need to get some bloody rest! 😊

Finally, numbers… Platelets really down, so will have some today. Red blood high now after a top-up. Immune system low and yet temperature totally fine! All part of the roller coaster, folks.

Take care, all.

Grandpa

26ᵗʰ October 2015

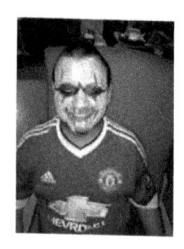

Caption: Thanks for the make-up tips, Daddy 😊 If you don't mind, I'll pass. Oh, and your mascara has run 😂 x

Good afternoon, everyone. So, let's tell you today's news on our little munchkin. Well, the tube is still in! So, thankfully, no distressing resiting issues today. The medical team have decided that to give her stomach a rest, they will give her TPN feeds. This is a feed that is so broken down, it can be given into the veins through her line and bypass the nose tube and stomach altogether. Given the pain she is in, they felt she needs a break – and we fully agree. It doesn't stop her eating when she wants to, it simply ensures she is receiving all the required goodies per day. Her general demeanour today is better than yesterday although she is receiving regular pain relief. There have even been the odd smile or two. They have morphine and horse tranquilisers on standby if the pain worsens. Yes, you read that right – it's totally true – same medication for horses! *Nay,* I hear you say! Hahaha 😂 We are still waiting for the blood results for today's numbers, but for now, it's about pain management, feeding and temperature, which, by the way, is over 38 and so it's back to antibiotics. I think you are starting to see the pattern now, folks. But hey, remember what I said yesterday – we are winning the war despite some pretty ugly battles.

Now I need to brief you all on Sorrelle's 1st birthday, which, as you may know, is on Thursday 29th October. And unless a miracle occurs, she will be celebrating it with her newfound nursey friends on the ward. As for what is happening…

Thursday – Cakes, gifts, and visits from those of you able to pop in before 8pm. No specific time, simply if you are around and able to. All I would say is, if there seems to be a fair few at any one time, we'll shift in and out of the ward. I imagine with work commitments, it'll be hard for most of you, and so we also have Sunday 1st November as a second opportunity to pop in and celebrate Sorrelle's 1st birthday, with cake.

Sunday – Again, no set times, so pop in and out throughout the day. Same rules about visiting ending at 8pm and shifting in and out if there are too many people at any one time. I am sure we will all get to see her.

So, we will keep a supply of cake on the go, and hopefully our little hero will be able to share a smile or two with us.

There will be lots of pictures and, of course, the daily update and caption. I hope you all saw earlier my request to tell the world. Let's see how many birthday messages we can get for her. The aim is to keep Mummy and Daddy busy all day reading them to her 😊

Well, that's all for today. Remember, the last chance to buy tickets for the hamper will be Wednesday 28th, and the draw will take place on Sorrelle's birthday.

Enjoy the picture

Grandpa

27ᵗʰ October 2015

Caption: Hey, Mummy, the smile is back. Let's show everybody ☺

Good evening, everyone. I think we would all agree that Saturday onwards was a pretty bad time. I'm sure you picked that up from my recent posts. Well, today, we turned a corner 😊 I am delighted to report lots of smiles, a lot less pain and the return of our delightful little hero. Now we know what to expect, next time won't be as much of a shock. We can plan for three to four days of crashing and then the start of recovery. She's receiving pain relief, and the new feed is proving to be far less intrusive and still giving her the goodies she needs. As for today's numbers, platelets are really low, and there will be a top-up tomorrow. Red count rose on its own today and, as before, this indicates recovery, or at least the start of. Immune system is still low, but the temp has returned to normal and so, all in all, her numbers are OK. In honesty, the most important thing is that, at least for now, Sorrelle is feeling much more like her old self. Just in time for her birthday on Thursday.

Hope this news brings a few more smiles and sighs of relief. She's doin' OK, folks 😊

Have a good evening.

Grandpa

28th October 2015

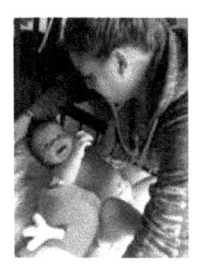

Caption: Hey mum, how are the birthday plans coming on

Good evening, everyone. So, it's birthday eve and time for an update. She's back 😊 Smiles, laughter, eating the odd bite and she's gained weight. Temperature has remained normal, and red blood and platelets have both started to rise on their own and so the recovery period is well under way – just in time for our little hero to enjoy her 1st birthday 😊 Lots of cake and gifts tomorrow and a repeat to come on Sunday.

Nothing more to add tonight, other than to remind you to get those birthday wish messages over tomorrow. It'll make lovely reading for Gem and Dean 😊

Have a great evening, everyone, and enjoy the pictures.

Grandpa

29th October 2015

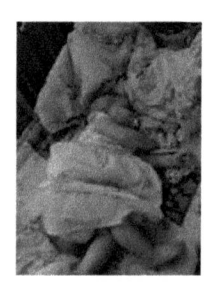

Caption: Well, Mummy and Daddy, I'm glad I only get one of these a year!

So are we, Munchkin, so are we! 😄 xx

Good evening, everyone. Time for the BIRTHDAY update :) Let's focus on a certain little girl's first birthday. It starts, of course, with the fact that she has the most amazing mummy and daddy in the world. As one of the old ones of the family, I'm pretty sure I can speak for all of us when I tell you, Gem and Dean, how incredibly proud of you we all are. Your courage, selflessness, love and determination are not only an inspiration to us but to your daughter too. How lucky she is, and will be, to know she has you both.

As for the little lady, well, they say a picture is worth a thousand words, so let's just look 😊 I have run out of words to adequately express our feelings for this remarkable little girl. What I can say, and what you can all see, is she has had the most amazing day. And she gets to do it all again on Sunday! To everyone out there who sent wishes, gifts, cards – you are all heroes and have my eternal gratitude. As you all know, my wish is that Gem and Dean take comfort from your comments on these posts and my requests to send wishes. You have made them smile – and shed the odd tear – and you are all playing such a crucial part in Sorrelle's battle and in their own journey. I am very proud of the army of family and friends out there. Angels, each and every one of you.

To the Slatterys – a huge thank you for the cupcakes you donated. Gemma and Dean were able to take them around the ward so every child had some cake and a party bag too.

The hospital's gift tonight, aside from the cake and a wonderfully sung 'Happy Birthday', are platelets and red blood as she's a little low 😊

Have a great evening, everyone, and again thank you.

Grandpa

30th October 2015

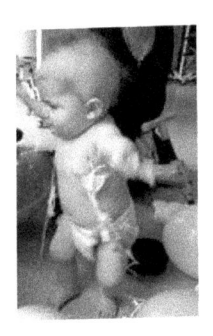

Caption: Let's look at that again. That's right, folks – no hands! X

Good evening, everyone. Well, Grandpa has the night shift tonight, so, naturally, my wonderful little granddaughter is, of course, going to sleep right through the night and let Grandpa rest! 😊 "Yeah right, Grandpa!"

Numbers today are OK as she has had top-ups of platelets and blood. She has, bless her, decided to play yo-yo with her temperature, though. She's currently at 38.9, like a little radiator. She's having a snooze at the moment and then I'm sure it'll be playtime again. Please don't worry about the temp – it happens all the time here. Be more concerned how horrific Grandpa's gonna look in the morning! Just in time for Halloween 😊

Have a good evening, everyone.

Enjoy the pictures and, of course, the captions.

31ˢᵗ October 2015

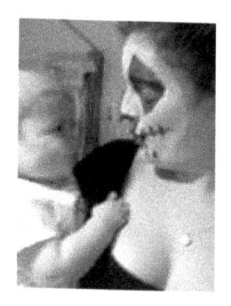

Caption: Hey, Mum, when you putting the face paint on? 😂 x

Good afternoon, everyone. Time for an update. Early, I know, but there are some bits of information to share with you all. First, we are waiting for the numbers for today as they haven't yet taken any blood. However, as I mentioned last time, our little munchkin is running a temperature. Initial results show she has picked up a bug, which is no surprise – it's a virus we all have in our bowel, but it can be resistant to certain antibiotics, so they just have to give her the right one. She is perfectly safe, and the bug is quite common in this situation – it's called VRE. She's a little warm and unsettled but sleeping at the moment.

The most important news is that she has to go into isolation. Visitors are still allowed but strictly only four around the bed at any one time. It's also essential you use hand gel on going in and out of the room to stop the bug from spreading. It isn't a risk to healthy children, only those with low immune systems, hence it being common on Ward 84. I say all this because, as you know, tomorrow is open house for people to come and see Sorrelle following her 1st birthday. This *can* still take place. You can still visit Sorrelle, but please remember, only four around the bed. I think it would make sense if you could comment here the kind of time you were planning on coming to see her. This way, everyone can see the times and what this might mean in terms of shuffling in and out. I'm afraid it won't be possible for us all to be in the room at the same time. We are sure that over the next 12 hours the right medications will start to help and that visitors will be perfectly fine. Apart from this, our little hero isn't too bad – just occasionally impersonating a radiator on number 4 😊

Enjoy the rest of your day.

Grandpa

So, it's 6:45am and the munchkin is fast asleep. The view from the ward is pretty spectacular for Manchester, and Grandpa looks like Grizzly Adams after a night out with the bears! Our little hero did the yo-yo thing with her temp and so has had paracetamol. She, of course, decided to wake up at 4:30am for what one can only describe as playtime! Aah, Munchie, it's a good job I love ya 😊 So, just been out for bread, Lurpak, jam, yogurts and milk to tempt our little angel when she wakes. In short, she's had a pretty settled night, even with the temp, whereas I'm off to find a couple of matchsticks

Have a great day, everyone, and I'll see you later for today's post.

PS Gem and Dean finally took a night at home! Hopefully many more to come, recharging those batteries and remembering time for each other. Hope you slept well, guys 😊

Even where we find ourselves, the world is still a pretty special place.

A very happy Grandpa

NOVEMBER 2015

2nd November 2015

Caption: I know, annoying, isn't it? I even look cute with pants on my head!

Good evening, everyone. And so today's news. First, the numbers. Red count and platelets are nice and steady and are beginning to increase without top-ups. Temperature is starting to normalise, hasn't gone over 38 since last night, so we think the antibiotics are now kicking in. As for the VRE, this has been confirmed but isn't responsible for the high temperatures, which are due to the infection in the line. As for her demeanour, totally fabulous – happy, smiley and laughing. There is even the possibility of going home in a week or two for a few days before the next round of chemotherapy.

One final piece of news… Our little hero, as of 4pm today, has a new cousin – Eliza May Price, weighing in at 9lb 1oz, to very proud and happy parents Matt and Beth 😊 So, all in all, a pretty good day, folks. Gem and Dean even got some time away in Manchester shopping. Dean is in recovery as we speak! Hahaha.

Have a great evening and enjoy the picture.

Grandpa

3rd November 2015

Caption: The challenge – look into my eyes and try not to think "cute" 😊
Good luck xx

Good evening, everyone. My apologies for the late update. I had the great honour of driving my new granddaughter home from the hospital tonight with her mummy and daddy. All is well in the world of Eliza 😊

Now to our little hero… As you can see from the pictures, I've simply gone cute tonight. She has had a really good day, aside from the trauma of tubes being inserted into her nose! Four attempts later, a fair few tears, and no more tubes. Gem is going to speak with the professor tomorrow and look at alternatives, especially as she has gained weight. Anyway, her numbers are stable and for the rest of the day there were equal measures of sleep and giggles. Day by day, she is recovering and although we know the cycle will start again soon, it's good to enjoy the good days. Our one-year-old little hero continues to show us the way with her bravery. Gem and Dean had some time to themselves today to meet their new niece and will be back at the hospital tomorrow. Really good and important that they are getting some time to unwind a little. As always to the army of friends and family out there, your wishes and comments continue to be a great source of strength to them, so thank you.

Well, folks, enjoy the pictures and, of course, captions.

Grandpa

4th November 2015

Caption: So you failed yesterday's challenge hahaha. This is so easy x

Good evening, everyone. Today's update. First, the numbers – red count over 100, platelets 142, temp normal. In short, really, really good 😊 Munchkin is recovering well after that first 10-day spell, and her numbers are increasing without the need for top-ups. Her smile is back big time and, as for eating, well, they're going to reduce the TPN feed (through a line) and then Sorrelle will start to feel hungry, and hopefully eat for herself. This should start in the next couple of days. This is one happy grandpa. Big granddaughter smiles just in time for Grandpa birthday cuddles tomorrow 😊

Hopefully more great days to follow before the next round of treatment, which we estimate will be in about a week's time.

Enjoy the picture from today.

Have a great evening.

Grandpa

5th November 2015

Caption: Hmm, washing your face, Daddy… Do you know what I've just done in here? 😂 No, Daddy, I mean it, I really have! It can only be one of two things – and it's not the first one, Daddy 😂

Good afternoon, everyone. Time for the Bonfire Night update. Maybe those fireworks are going off to celebrate the great news that Munchie gets some freedom tomorrow! Yes, that's right, she's going home 🙂 Just for a few days until the bone marrow test next Wednesday. Obviously, this suggests her numbers are steadily improving, added to which she is eating more for herself now. Gem and Dean are over the moon. It'll be so good to have a little family time at home. I'm sure you will see the evidence of her eating in one of the pictures – it's all around her mouth! A really good day – better sleeping, better numbers, better eating, and home tomorrow. It's as good as it gets, folks.

Enjoy the pictures. Have a great Guy Fawkes Night and hope you enjoy the caption. I know you will.

Can I also say a quick but heartfelt thank you for all the lovely birthday wishes today 🙂

Grandpa

6th November 2015

Caption: Cute goes home 😊 xx

Good evening, everyone. Time for tonight's update and it's a short one… SHE'S HOME! 😊 Her numbers today are fine, and the final blood tests this morning confirmed she could spend the weekend at home. As we speak, Sorrelle is tucked up with Mummy and Daddy, enjoying some long overdue family time. Back to hospital on Monday to check levels and prepare for the next bone marrow test but, for now, let's all enjoy the weekend, knowing our little hero is once again doing her thing and amazing us all.

Have a great weekend, everyone, and watch out for the weekend picture that will appear at some point 😊

Grandpa

7th November 2015

Caption: Is it me or does my smile seem even brighter at home? 😊 x

Good evening, everyone. Today's news is simply that, medically, there is absolutely no news – which is great 😊 The reason for that, of course, is our little hero is enjoying Mummy and Daddy time at home and visiting Grandma and Pops 😊 The pictures say it far better than I could, so I shall leave you all to enjoy your evenings.

See you at the next post!

Grandpa x

8th November 2015

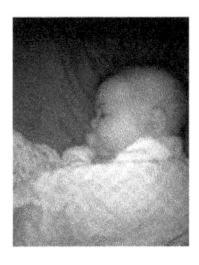

Caption: Wow, I don't remember home life being sooo tiring 😊 x

Good afternoon, everyone. Well, Sunday at home was pretty much like Saturday – smiles, mischief and family time. Sorrelle's temperature has stayed totally normal throughout, and she's eaten more and had lots of the formulated/enriched milk from the hospital to maintain and increase her weight. Gem and Dean are enjoying being at home. Initially, they were really relaxed, though once our little hero started to step up the mischief, the relaxation went west! Ah, the joys of parenthood 😊 Most importantly, this is the most time at home they've had since the diagnosis back in August! Has it been that long already? 😳

Tomorrow, it's back to hospital for tests, just to make sure her counts are high enough to do the bone marrow test and LP on Wednesday. All part of the routine, ahead of the next 10-day treatment, which we reckon will start next Monday, maybe earlier depending on the results.

Not much more to report other than to take a moment to thank you all once again for your continued support for Gem and Dean. You may see the difference you're making in the pictures but even if you don't, please rest assured you are.

Grandpa

9th November 2015

Caption: Choo choo! All that's missing is Jimmy, Auntie Rachel.

Good evening, everyone. Time for today's update. Hospital visit today to check counts. Results were excellent – red count over 100 and rising without medication, platelets over 500, which is amazing, temperature still normal and immune system rising. The professor is delighted, and consequently Sorrelle has been allowed home again until the bone marrow test on Wednesday and then home again until next Monday, when the next round of treatment begins. Can't tell you what a great boost this is for Gem and Dean. Family normality, dinners, bedtime stories, baths, watching her sleep in her own bed – those things we take for granted and yet are special. Really good times, folks, that we can all take comfort from and enjoy.

Have a great evening, everyone. I'm pretty sure a certain little girl will 😊

Grandpa

10th November 2015

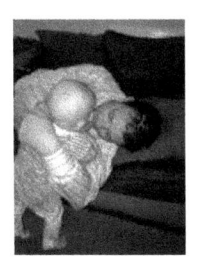

Caption: Wake up, Grandpa. You've got my post to write.

Evening, everyone. Well, we are now in the 12th week since diagnosis. We know our little hero is winning the battle against this horrible disease, but what continues to amaze me is how. Still the smiles, always wanting to be happy, and I'm sure she knows it makes us happy too. Almost seems she's helping us more than we're helping her 😊

Today was another fun day with Katie and Ila. Lots of smiles and quality time. Days like this are important, not just for Sorrelle but for all of us. They give us all a little normality. Back into hospital tomorrow for the bone marrow test and LP, so a little sleep through the procedures, then hopefully she can return home until the next round of treatment starts. I will keep you all posted tomorrow as to how things went and confirm when she'll be re-admitted.

In the meantime, enjoy these smiles, have a good evening, and thank you for your continued support for Gem, Dean and Sorrelle. You are all playing such an important part in this journey.

Grandpa

11th November 2015

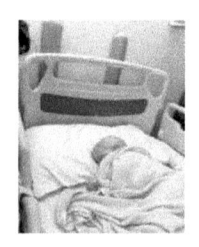

Caption: A small boat in a big bed 😊 x

Good evening, everyone. Well, bone marrow test and LP done. Results tomorrow. The little munchkin had a bit of sickness today after the procedure, so stayed in hospital for a few hours. She had a sleep, a little toast when she woke up, and I have just dropped her with Mummy and Daddy at home. The next round of chemotherapy will start on Friday not Monday. Sorrelle is so well now, we want to give this disease the next blow while we can. So, a couple of nights at home and then the journey continues. Still smiling, as you can see 😊

Have a good evening, everyone.

Grandpa

12th November 2015

Caption: Sat in Asda, next to the stock. Only thing missing is the price tag! 😊 x

Good evening, everyone. Hope you are all well. So, it's treatment eve. Tomorrow back to the hospital for the next round of chemotherapy. The breaks at home are wonderful for Gem and Dean and, of course, for Sorrelle, but the truth is, the normality for the next two years is treatment regimes, with the odd few days at home. It's so easy to lose yourself when you have that glimpse of home life that it then makes going back into hospital tough. I'm sure Gem and Dean are gonna be feeling that, so it's up to us, folks, to keep those messages of encouragement coming, especially tonight. As for how our little hero is … pretty damn good really 😊 Eating up a storm for the first time in a while, and those smiles are there for all to see.

Well, everyone, will post again tomorrow and give you the latest info, on day one of the new round of treatment.

Grandpa

13th November 2015

Caption: What? I'm hungry x

Good evening, everyone. So, our little hero is once again on Ward 84, wowing them all. The professor used the word 'excellent' when describing her results from Wednesday. This is why she's in early for treatment – we're striking while the iron's hot, so to speak.

She had chicken nuggets and fries today and loved them 😊 We've been treated to a few days of great smiles and good health. Now the cycle starts again. We know the first seven or eight days of treatment are OK and then it'll be a struggle, so let's get ourselves ready and keep those messages coming for Gem and Dean to enjoy 😊

Enjoy the picture.

Grandpa

14ᵗʰ November 2015

Caption: Anyone receiving me? Houston, we have a problem 😊 x

Good evening, everyone. You will remember me telling you when I started doing these posts, that I wouldn't lie to you about any news we have. We know there are gonna be good days and bad days. Today is a bad day. Temperature has been over 40 a fair few times and has remained over 38 all day. She's being given pain relief and antibiotics and, bless her, she's not herself tonight. Struggling to sleep with the discomfort she's in. Today's chemotherapy is another new one, and it may be that her body has to get used to it. We just have to be strong and help her through it. We've been here before, so please don't worry that this is in some way more serious – it honestly isn't, and she will start to improve.

Let's please keep the messages coming for Gem and Dean. Reckon they could really do with them. The crazy thing is, her immune system has never been higher – and her red count and platelets are really high. We are on that roller coaster for sure!

Take care, people.

Grandpa

15th November 2015

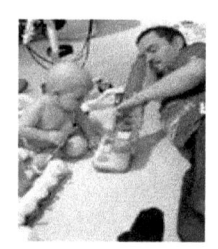

Caption: Look, Dad, I've done three of them for you just to make it easier! Come on, shape up 😊 x

Good evening, all. Time for the Sorrelle news 😊 Well, still not great today. Although her temperature has had spells under 38, it's prone to spiking and, as we speak, it's rising again. On the eating front, she's tried a little, which is good. Obviously, she hasn't exactly feasted, but I suspect we wouldn't either if we were feeling ill.

As you can see from today's pictures, our little hero doesn't seem too interested in much, but again, would we be? On a positive note, she is still coping with it – and far better than I would be, that's for sure. And she's still beating it. We're another day closer to ringing that bell. She did manage a little time out of her cot today, so I've used that picture as today's caption 😊

As always, thank you for all your messages. I have to say how moved I am by your constant stream of support and for never wavering from helping whenever I ask. So, from me to all of you, a very sincere and heartfelt thank you.

Have a good evening, all.

Grandpa

16th November 2015

Caption: No, Grandpa, I disagree. If I pull it hard enough, I think it'll come off 😂 x

Good afternoon, everyone. Well, today's news is a little better thankfully 😊 A few little bits to eat and, most importantly, her temperature has stayed normal today. Red blood count is low, so there will be a top-up tonight. Immune system is OK and platelets are still high. Last night was a bit uncomfortable for her, but today has been better. Hopefully, after some blood tonight, she'll have a better night. We even had some smiles today and a little more activity 😊

Pictures have just been taken, so they're the latest.

Have a good evening, all.

Grandpa

17th November 2015

Caption: Psst. Come a little closer. I know he's behind me, so I'll have to whisper. I've been showing him how to use this all afternoon! Guess where he's up to. D – E – A – N! Yes, Dad, well done! You've typed your name :) Dads today, eh! 😂 x

Good afternoon, everyone. Today's news is not too bad actually. Went to Manchester shopping and Sorrelle has put on weight 😊 Bloods nice and high and clearly getting used to the treatment this time round. Her immune system's dropping but was high enough today to get off the ward, which was a huge bonus 😊

Nothing to report, other than one important announcement. As you can see in the pictures, Sorrelle is checking out a laptop for kids' games and watching DVDs on. Gem and Dean would like to thank all of you out there for this. A bit of the money you are so kindly raising and donating to help make their lives a little easier has just been spent on this. Given Sorrelle has to spend so much time in hospital, this piece of kit will help fill some of the hours before she gets out. You cannot imagine the huge difference little things like this make, so have yourselves a self-pride moment as this is what you have been able to do 😊 Thanks everyone from Sorrelle too.

Oh, and enjoy the caption. Dean sure will. Haha. Yep, you guessed it, Dean. You again 😂 That's what dads are for. Trust me, I know 😂

Grandpa

18th November 2015

Caption: Oh, that's just great. Lumber me with these two! Well, of course, THEY'RE smiling. They have me 😂 At least I don't have to smile to be cute 😂 x

Good evening, everyone. So, numbers first of all. Red blood count dropping and will probably need a top-up tomorrow. Temperature has been OK, spiked a little, and they found she has an ear infection. Nothing to worry about – a course of antibiotics will sort it out pretty quick. Platelets are nice and high, and all in all Munchkin is coping a little better now. The reason this set of treatment hit her hard at the start is that it was a full dose rather than the usual smaller ones. The last treatment of this cycle will be on Monday, and we expect her to be a little rough for a few days. All part of the roller coaster we are learning about so well.

As you can see, Sorrelle is pretty good now. Had a painting day today 😊 Food has been so-so – could always be better – but, hey, little steps along the road are better than none.

Enjoy the picture folks.

Have a good evening.

Grandpa

19th November 2015

Caption: And you all thought Grandpa typed the posts 😊 x

Good afternoon, all. The latest instalment of the Sorrelle news. Her immune system – well, basically, there isn't one 😨 Because of the infection, her red count is low but not so low to need top-ups. Temp is normal, but food once again seems to be an issue. Have been tempting her with a variety of food 😊 Today's pictures clearly show Munchkin to be happy enough.

Not much more to say. Treatment is still going OK and she seems to be coping better as the days go by.

Caption to follow.

Have a good evening, all.

Grandpa

20th November 2015

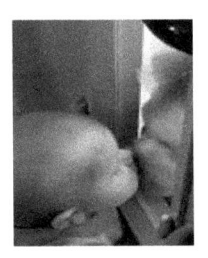

Caption: Mirror, mirror, on the wall... Oh my God, I've turned into me mother! 😂 x

Good evening, everyone. Time to give you today's update. Well, it was a bit of a rough night, with a fair bit of sickness. Unsure yet if it's the antibiotics from the ear infection or the chemo or a bit of both, but in any event she will need fluids later. Her numbers are all falling, but please remember we expect this as we near the end of this round of treatment. And, of course, they can top up platelets and blood. As for her immune system, it's pretty much on the floor, and her weight today shows a loss. They do think the weight may be incorrect, so no tube feeds just yet, though there are likely to be in the next few days. Seems similar to last time, if we cast our minds back. The good news is, despite all this, she finds strength from somewhere – God knows where – to still smile and treat us all to yet more examples of that cheeky sense of fun. As I have said many times before, I sometimes think she helps us through this more than we help her 😊

Enjoy the picture. Tonight's caption is pretty good and pretty clever, even if I do say so myself 😂

Take care, everyone.

Grandpa

21st November 2015

Caption: Today we need smiles xx

Good evening, everyone. Today's update. Sorry to say it's not been a good day. Her numbers are falling, but that's to be expected. I'm referring to her generally. She's been sick throughout the day and so is having fluids through the line. She's very quiet, almost motionless, and is running between hot and cold. She had to have a nose tube put in earlier, which was very unsettling for her, and a little later she pulled it out and had to have it redone. Aside from waiting for results to see if she has a bug, the professor isn't overly concerned about these symptoms. Basically, she's been hit by all the typical side effects of her condition. We simply have to wait it out, which, if I'm honest, is upsetting. I've always told you I would be honest with you – and I am. It goes without saying that messages to Gemma and Dean would be especially welcome today.

I want to finish with something a little more positive. First, Sorrelle will be OK. And second, I want to tell you all about the most amazing nurse. When Sorrelle needed the nose tube redoing, this wonderful nurse gave her a bottle so the swallowing motion would make passing the tube less distressing. Not only did this work wonderfully, but Sorrelle almost didn't even notice. Simple thing like this, yet total genius! First time we've seen this. It's proof, if ever it were needed, that we are blessed with the most amazing people caring for Sorrelle. This nurse especially is the very definition of care and compassion. I would like you all, when you message Gemma, to say a little thank you to this angel of a nurse. I want her to know just how special she is and how grateful we are that Sorrelle is in her care.

Pictures today, as you can see, show our little hero has the odd bad day too. Caption to follow.

Take care, everyone.

Grandpa

22nd November 2015

Caption: Just want to say to my cuz, sorry I missed your party and happy 1st birthday for tomorrow.

Good afternoon, everyone. Hope you are all well. A bit more of that bumpy road today, I'm afraid. Sorrelle has septicaemia. She's having antibiotics and fluids and has been quite unwell, but she's stable. ICU will take her to provide more support if she needs it, but for now she's still on the ward. Her other numbers are irrelevant tonight – the priority is to treat the septicaemia. This is obviously a worry for us all, but she's in the right place, getting the best treatment from the best team we could ask for. Say a word for our little hero. I am sure she will fight this, just as she has everything else nature has cruelly thrown at her.

The pictures are from today, and you can see she has a little more colour than yesterday. There isn't anything else I can tell you because she isn't really doing anything other than lying still, with the very occasional smile.

I would like to thank you all for last night's messages. They were such a comfort, and that amazing nurse I told you about got to hear them. I hope we didn't embarrass her too much.

Caption to follow.

Grandpa

23rd November 2015

Caption: Mummy, when I said I wanted a foot-long Subway, that's not what I meant.

Good afternoon, all. And so on with the story so far. First, the chemotherapy – she's now had her last dose for this round and so we can focus on the infection. Cultures show the septicaemia is from one of the lines in her chest that she gets her medication through. They've identified what antibiotics to administer and will continue with fluids. If she shows no improvement by Wednesday, they'll remove the lines. Her ear infection has responded to antibiotics, though I have to say, with the amount she's having, she should be the healthiest person in here!

What we can tell you is, for the first time in days, she sat up. It was only for a few minutes, but after the stillness of the last few days, this is massive. She's still nil by mouth as her bowel needs rest and they need to stop her vomiting – which is working. To make sure she's nourished, they will put her on TPN feeding, which is done through the lines.

She's still sleeping a lot and has little energy, but as the medication kicks in, I hope to be able to tell you she's improving. It seems we're over the worst, so long as there are no relapses.

Take care, all.

Grandpa

24th November 2015

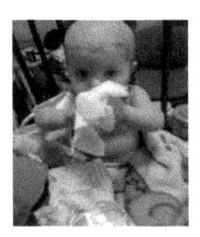

Caption: So, you heard they won't give me any food ... How tasty are tissues! 😊 x

Good evening, everyone. If we were to sum up today in two words, it would be 'stable' and 'sleep'! Two words which, quite frankly, after the last few days, are pretty good words to write! Again, we're not really focusing on numbers today, although her temperature has remained normal for over 24 hours, which is a good sign. We know that, medically, things can change quickly – it's almost as though there should be some kind of disclaimer like you get on stock market transactions, where your investment can go up and down! But our little hero is once again coming up trumps and carrying on the good fight 😊 Where she gets the courage from, I don't know, but we're sure glad she does. As for the septicaemia, it looks as though things are still moving forward. She does, however, seem to have what we think is mucositis in her stomach, which is making her a bit sick. This is a side effect of the chemotherapy, and it will pass. Until it does, they will only let her be line fed.

As you can see from the pictures, she is trying, bless her. Keep crossing those fingers, folks – it seems to be working 😊

Enjoy the picture.

Grandpa

25th November 2015

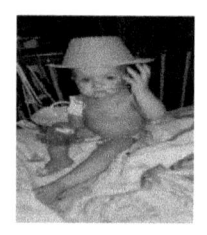

Caption: OK, Mum and Dad, the hat thing stops now! Or I'm putting in a report to those child cruelty people 😂 By the way, Mum, Dad hasn't used this one, has he? 😂

Good evening, everyone. And so today's news. Again, we'll leave the numbers for tonight, other than to say her temperature's normal, her platelets are very low and are being topped up, and her immune system … well, there isn't one! Aside from that, today's pictures show smiles! Boy, have we missed those! Still no food to rest her stomach and bowel and still under antibiotics for the infection, but it would seem her recovery is under way. I realise when we say this something usually comes along and kicks us in the teeth, but let's just take the good bits when they come. The all-important MRD test results come back at the beginning of next week, which will tell us the percentage of cancer cells that need removing and whether to continue chemotherapy or whether she needs a bone marrow transplant. In any event, we'll know the way forward. The next step is for her to recover and to be allowed to try some food.

Enjoy the picture, folks, and have a good evening.

Grandpa

26th November 2015

Good evening, all. Hope you are all well. As for our little hero, a better day 😃 Blood count is good, platelets low but OK. Immune system … what immune system! And temperature normal for most of the day, although it did spike high once, which is normal some days after treatment. She's a little more active, there have been more smiles – which I've missed like crazy – and she's even tried to eat a little. The eating will need to be introduced slowly for her stomach to tolerate it.

There isn't much more to tell you. We are now in recovery time, and the next treatment will be around Christmas. Let's all keep everything crossed for good news from the results next Monday.

Grandpa

27th November 2015

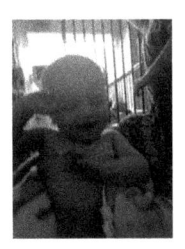

Caption: Come on, Mummy. Shake it, sister 😄 *Boogie woogie!*

Good evening, everyone. Today's update. A little blue, really. That's Manchester City blue! A visit from Manchester City Youth team and Patrick Vieira – a lovely tonic 😃 Our little hero, as you can see, is steadily improving, and we reckon over the next two or three days she'll be much more her old self. It seems no matter what Mother Nature and medicine throw at her, she keeps bouncing back 😃 Her numbers today are stable enough and she had a few hours without tubes and a little more room to move. The antibiotics continue to fight any infections lurking, and we wait for Monday/Tuesday and those all-important MRD results. Really hoping the little munchkin is well enough to celebrate her mummy's birthday on Sunday. The main area to work on is food, though to everyone's surprise, she's gained weight! This is hugely important in the fight of this disease, and hopefully over the next few days she'll eat more for herself.

A pretty good day all round and a nice way to send us off into the weekend. Have a great weekend, everyone. And for Sorrelle's family over in America, we're all sending you a special wish for a happy Thanksgiving.

Grandpa

28th November 2015

Caption: So, it lights up, it projects, it changes colour… But make it fly, Grandpa, make it fly.

Good evening, everyone. Tonight's update is a pretty good one, just to prepare you 😊 Simply take a look at tonight's pictures. A picture is worth a thousand words, as they say. The sparkle is back. Not just the smile but that unmistakable Sorrelle twinkle 😊 Have to tell you, folks, it's a joy to see. As you can guess, I'm on the night shift tonight, and if last night's 12-hour sleep is anything to go by, then I reckon I've picked a good night.

She's a little low on red count and platelets and so there will be a top-up tonight. It looks as though she's over the infections, and her temperature has remained great. You can also see she's enjoying a nap after playtime with Grandpa. When she wakes, we're gonna try some noodles 😊 She's really in pretty good shape, and although these good news posts always come with an understanding that things can and do change, let's hold onto today and let it shape the remainder of our weekends. Take a deep breath, smile, and enjoy your families.

Take care, all.

Grandpa

PS Have a great night out, Gemjar and Dean, on your birthday eve 😊 x

29th November 2015

Good afternoon, everyone. Today's update will make you smile. And, believe me, today's caption may even have you shed a tear. You don't want to miss it. (Alas in video format)

But first, today's news. Well, following a great night's sleep, Sorrelle woke up smiling, with no temperature, topped up with blood and platelets, and has quite simply been a joy 😊 I had lots of cuddles and we even had a few Chinese noodles together. Then this morning, she had a little "Daddy breakfast" that I made for Gem for her birthday. Since her temperature's settled, it looks like the antibiotics can stop, and she can recover fully from the last round of treatment. As you can see from today's pictures, she is well on the way to that. Our little munchkin is back on top form just in time for her mum's birthday 😊 There isn't anything else to add, especially as I want to get the caption on quick. We need to give massive thanks to Dean's uncle, who is responsible for today's caption. It's amazing!

Take care, all.

Grandpa

30th November 2015

Caption: Hmm, chicken nuggets. I've missed these x

Good evening, everyone. So, here we are, 14 weeks in. As you can see, that smile is still there. Despite months of treatment, temperatures, infections, septicaemia, sickness and general yuck, our little hero marches on beating this horrible disease. We're still waiting for the MRD results, which determine the next treatment, but right now she's in a good place and her body's improving daily. Once her immune system's recovered, who knows, maybe some more time at home. At this time of year, we're all hoping that time at home is a reality, but equally we don't want to build up hope. But so far so good 😊 As for her numbers, they're pretty constant – low and improving. Gem and Dean are still battling on and are in a pretty good place at the moment and coping with all of this remarkably well. We should all be proud of them both. I get to see, almost daily, their commitment to each other – not just to Sorrelle.

Once again, your messages really do make a difference, and they all get read.

Well, not much more to report today, other than to wish you all a pleasant evening. Enjoy the smiley pictures and that sparkle in her eyes.

Grandpa

DECEMBER 2015

1st December 2015

Caption: I think, therefore I am 😊 x

Good evening, everyone. I know it's a little late tonight, but I took Gemma to watch the Manchester City game 😊 Now we've returned to the hospital, it's time to give you all an update. Well, we won 4-1, had loads of possession… Oh, sorry, wrong news 😂 Munchkin, of course 😊

Her numbers today were low and so she's had a top-up of blood and platelets. Her temperature's spiked a few times today and it appears that once again there's an infection in her line. So that will be removed tomorrow. Antibiotics should help fight it. She's happy in herself, though a little irritable with the temperature. She did, however, manage to tuck into some food earlier and she's trying to settle, as I speak.

Well, not much more to tell you, folks. Again, apologies for the late post.

Grandpa

2nd December 2015

Caption: Oh, great warrior princess, Daddy bows to your greatness. And after my adventures, I have returned to honour thy greatness with a gift of ... a giant fluffy penguin! 😄 x

Good afternoon, everyone. And so today's update. Pretty slow news day to be honest. Medically, very little change, which, based on the last few days, is a good thing. She's in great spirits and her temperature has returned to normal. The cultures from yesterday show she's clear of infection, so things are calming down nicely. Not too much happened today with food, but I expect she'll try a little something later. She's currently sleeping sweetly following an afternoon of playing and a visit from Uncle Matt 😊

She's also had a little dance, which you will see on a video I have for you, in addition to today's caption.

Well, folks, have a good evening and enjoy the picture and caption.

Grandpa

3rd December 2015

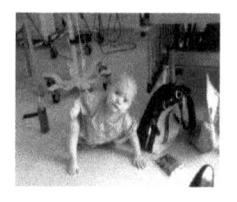

Caption: Erm, Mummy and Daddy, a quick question... You haven't seen a spare leg lying around here, have you? ☺

4th December 2015

Caption: Hey, Grandpa, I've just noticed two things ... I'm VERY cute and you are VERY small 😂 x

Good evening, everyone. And so to today's update on our little hero. Let's get the worrying bit out of the way first – the all-important MRD test results we've been waiting for. If we're honest, they're kinda mixed, which I know sounds strange, so I'll try to explain. When Sorrelle went into remission, there was no sign of leukaemia in her bone marrow. At that point, they did a chromosome test to detect levels of cancer cells left in her body. This initially measured at 1%, which sounds low and easily treatable. The truth is, this is the most difficult bit to get rid of – and the chromosome test is not very accurate. So, when a second chromosome test done a few weeks ago showed 1% also, the professor requested this MRD test – which is VERY accurate. This MRD result is higher than 1%. In fact, it's 3%. Our natural reaction was that things are worse, but because the chromosome tests are so inaccurate it may have been 3% all along. We will never know. So, what does all this mean? It means that Sorrelle still has cancer cells, and it will still take two years to beat this thing.

The next stage is for the professor to get some other opinions over the next few days and then adjust the treatment plan accordingly. What we do know is that 3% is too high to do a bone marrow transplant, so that is off the table for now. I know you may feel worried about this, but I urge you to remember nothing has really changed – she is still here, still in remission, still receiving treatment, still laughing, still giggling, still wowing the nurses and still throwing in the occasional mischief just for Mum and Dad 😊 Of course, we would have loved the MRD to say

0.5%, but even if it had, the treatment is still two years. So, as I said, nothing's really changed.

I do think it's still a good day to send Gem and Dean a message or two. A little moral support right now would be very welcome. This roller coaster ride won't be an easy one, and there will be good days and bad days. And days when you don't know what to think – I think today is one of those days. So, the best tonic is to take a look at tonight's picture and the caption and find yourselves smiling at that gorgeous little hero 😊

I've been totally honest with you – you know what we know. As soon as we get an update on the revised treatment plan, we will let you know.

Have a good weekend, everyone, and please do send those messages. They really are a help.

Grandpa

5th December 2015

Caption: My wonderful public – a girl's gotta sleep, ya know.

Good evening, everyone. This evening's update. Not too much to say really. I'm on the night shift tonight, so I get the company of this amazing little girl all night. Her numbers today are still low and not yet started to recover on their own, so more platelets, as we speak. Her temp has just gone to 38 again and so we all know what that means – back on the antibiotics! She's still a chirpy soul, though the picture tonight is last night's, due in no small part to her being fast asleep 😊 She watched that Christmas song again and again, had a cuddle from Grandpa and fell asleep in my arms. I am so lucky to get these good bits 😊 She will wake a little later for a play and maybe some food and then we'll probably have a peaceful night. Gem and Dean are home for the night, which they need badly.

Well, enjoy your evening, everyone.

Grandpa

6th December 2015

Caption: Mummy, I know Grandpa said you should be behind bars, but where do I sleep? ☺

Good evening, everyone. Well, I'm back after a lovely evening with our little hero. She slept pretty well last night and woke up around 8am, spent an hour or so playing, then slept again. Her temperature's been spiking and she's been sick a few times – all signs of infection – and so she's being given a pretty strong antibiotic, to try and kill it off before it gets a chance to take hold. Again, on the food front, nothing to report, which isn't good, but we should bear in mind that if we had a bug, we wouldn't want to eat either. Basically, the sooner these bugs stop and her counts start to recover naturally, the sooner the Sorrelle we all know and love will be back. She's been sleeping a lot over the last couple of days, which suggests there's something going on. Despite all this, she's happy enough in herself, though a little pale and quiet. There will be a meeting with the professor tomorrow to discuss the way forward following the MRD but, more immediately, to get her recovery stepped up a gear. Well, that's it for now, folks. Enjoy your evening.

Grandpa

7th December 2015

Good evening, everyone. Time for tonight's update. First, our little munchkin's numbers. Erm … they're LOW! Needs more platelets tonight and her immune system is still very low, which means she's especially open to infection. And she isn't disappointing us there! She's had a fair few of them – and has another as we speak. Temperature is still over 38 and so the antibiotics continue.

Gem and Dean had a chance to speak at length with the professor as to the treatment options following the MRD result, and so the plan is as follows… Continue the recovery period from this last treatment for the next 2/3 weeks, then get results of more MRD tests, and then in a few weeks, the next round of chemotherapy. Although it will be an intensive treatment, it will be a different drug to see if the response is better/faster than the previous one. Again, I must remind you that all this information and the subtle changes in treatment don't change the fundamental parameters; namely, that this is a two-year process. Once this next round of treatment is completed, they will assess the results and, only change plans if they need to. For now, everyone, we just carry on as before.

As you can see from the pictures, even though her counts are low, she's looking the picture of cuteness 😊 It's all about treatment recovery phase now, and hopefully in the next week or two, she should start creating her own platelets and red count again. I have to say, getting any time at home for Christmas is looking remote, so we will see that as a big bonus if it happens. This way, we won't get too disappointed.

Take care, all.

Grandpa

8th December 2015

Caption: Hey, Daddy, this invisible chess is a great idea!

Good evening, everyone. And so today's post. To be honest, not a great night for our little hero. High temperature, high heart rate, low oxygen, not much sleep – all down to the treatment. The inevitable infections don't help, nor do the low blood count and platelets, both of which have been topped up tonight. Still a time of antibiotics and waiting, which is frustrating for us all, but I suspect if Sorrelle could tell us, she would say it's pretty frustrating for her. Penguins of Madagascar is pretty much on loop! Hahaha.

In the meantime, we just carry on. I promise you all in a week or two we'll be back to sparkling eyes and mischief 😊 Hope you enjoy tonight's pictures. Not many action shots today, and I've had to raid the archives for tonight's caption picture.

Have a good evening, all. Grandpa

9th December 2015

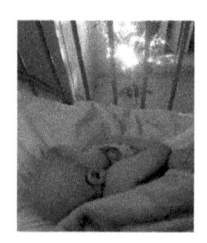

Caption: Yes, Munchkin, Christmas will still be here when you wake up. Sweet dreams, little one x

Evening, all. Well, what a difference a day makes! That with platelets and blood! As you can see, the colour is coming back, along with that fun, mischievous girl 😊 Looks like the counts are starting to show the first signs of recovering. We suspect her sparkle will be here real soon. Glad to report her temperature's starting to settle. Obviously, the antibiotics and paracetamol are helping with this, but in the next few days, I reckon our little hero will be well on her way.

Tonight, she had a play in the bath and some stories, along with those penguins again! Nothing much else to report. We've grown to realise that sometimes no news can be very good news 😊

Enjoy the picture, folks.

Grandpa

10th December 2015

Caption: See, everyone – I smile because I have such a pretty, ladylike mummy 😊
x

Good evening, everyone. Today's news is pretty brief as we're still on our way to count recovery. Our little munchkin needs blood and platelets today, but at least it's not every day now, which means the counts are getting better. And today's pictures certainly show that fun is back. We also have an immune system (just, ha ha) but we're on the right track. She's getting a little more time not hooked up, which helps her play and is great for cuddles 😊

Not much more to say, other than thank you for reading these posts and for your supportive and loving comments.

Have a good evening.

Grandpa

11th December 2015

Caption: A little reminder what cute looks like – and I don't mean Grandpa 😊

x

Good evening, everyone. My apologies for the delay. Grandpa has had some time out this evening with work colleagues to celebrate the festive season. I did call in to see our little hero, and the news is pretty good again. She seems very happy, and counts are still on that upward curve. She's lost a little weight and so she's getting all the goodies she needs through her line. We do think her back teeth are coming through, which might explain her lack of eating, but we expect she'll want to eat more once she feels better. You can see she's chilled out on her penguin beanbag this evening 😊

All in all, things are moving in the right direction.

Take care, all.

Grandpa

12th December 2015

Caption: One of my favourite cute pictures x

Good evening, everyone. You'll be pleased to know there isn't much to report tonight, other than the little monkey deciding to run a temperature and being back on antibiotics. She is, however, smiling lots and the counts, though falling, are doing so at an ever-slowing rate, which is good news. Still need to get the little munchkin to eat more, but for now count recovery is key and that is going OK.

A visit from Auntie Rachel and cousin Arthur was a lovely surprise, though it took Sorrelle a little getting used to as she hasn't interacted with other children since isolation started.

Well, nothing more to report at this point. Have a lovely evening.

Grandpa

13th December 2015

Caption: I'm puckered up and ready. Go on, give us a kiss 😊 x

Good evening, everyone, and welcome to the cheeky faces of Sorrelle 😊 As you can see, our little munchkin seems quite happy. As for today's numbers, well, she is, as we speak, having a blood top-up and, based on the platelet levels, I'm guessing she'll need a top-up tomorrow. They're getting further apart, which means her treatment recovery is slow but moving in the right direction. One of the things they mentioned is that, as the treatments continue, it'll take longer for count recovery because of the cumulative effect. Her immune system's still very low and her temperature's pretty normal at the moment. Food is still an issue and, consequently, she's on TPN feeding, which is not into the stomach. The flip side of this is that because it makes her feel full, she doesn't want to eat. But she'd lost weight and so she had to go onto it. As always, she's feeling pretty good in herself, so we'll take that 😊

That's about it for tonight. Hope you've had a good weekend.

Take care, all.

Grandpa

14th December 2015

Caption: Use the force, Luke. Use the force 😄 x

Good evening, all. Tonight's news is pretty brief, and that's because the news is getting better 😊 As you can see, she's looking as gorgeous as ever and is filled with cuteness 😊 Her numbers are steadily improving, and we had the magic 'home' word today. Antibiotics have stopped, her weight has increased, and we're keeping everything crossed for Christmas at home. It's a long shot but, hey, why not reach for the stars. Some work to do with normal eating, but she'll get the hang of it again.

Hope you enjoy the pictures. Take care, all.

Grandpa

15th December 2015

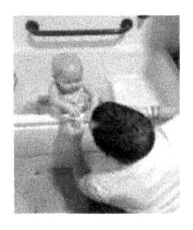

Caption: Yes, Daddy, you must always be lower than royalty 😄 x

Good evening, everyone. Late one and a quick one tonight. Our little hero has just eaten pizza with Grandpa! 😊 Yes, that recovery is well under way. Numbers are looking good and as the video earlier suggested, she's a very happy little girl. A good day today 😊

Take care.

Grandpa

16th December 2015

Caption: Oh boy, Daddy, you've really done it this time 😊 Spot the odd one out x

Good evening, everyone. So, where to begin? Yogurt, toast, chocolate buttons, chicken nuggets, chips, burger buns – yes, that's right, folks, it's not a shopping list but the items our little hero has been munching on throughout the course of the day 😊 You would therefore be right in thinking that she's had a pretty good day. And her numbers are stabilising nicely. Who knows – those crossed fingers might just get her home for Christmas Day 😊 Oh, did I mention she even had a very special visit today? Manchester City FC thank you for your kindness.

Have a lovely evening, all.

Grandpa

17th December 2015

Caption: Yeah, 'cos you've been busy all day, Dad! X

Good evening, everyone. So, how about some pretty good news… She's going home! Tomorrow or Saturday the medics reckon. Her numbers are going in the right direction and will be good enough to let her home. Amazing news. And, with a little check-up next Wednesday, the munchkin should be enjoying Christmas at home. I don't think we need to say anything else.

Have a great evening, everyone.

Grandpa

18th December 2015

Caption: Hey, Mummy and Daddy. Thanks for your bed … this is cosy 😁 *x*

Good evening, everyone. A short update tonight and just the one picture for a very good reason. You are looking at our little hero asleep in Mummy's bed! She is finally home and can stay home until Boxing Day. She will pop back to the hospital on Wednesday just to check count levels and top up if needed. So, as long as her temperature stays normal, it's going to be quite a special Christmas.

What I'd like to do, with your permission, is do the next post on Monday. Let's leave Gem, Dean and Sorrelle to some well-earned private time. After four months of living life under a microscope, I'm sure it will do them all good to even tell Grandpa to get lost for a couple of days 😁 As we close this post, let me, on behalf of Gem and Dean, thank you for all the wonderful messages of support and the abundance of love you have shown. They are indeed blessed to have such a warm, loving army of family and friends. You are making this journey much more bearable for them.

Have a fantastic weekend, all, and I'll update you on Monday.

Grandpa

21st December 2015

Caption: Hey, Dad, where have you put the beers? 😂 x

Evening, everyone. As promised, update time. They say a picture is worth a thousand words and so, put simply, this is what a great weekend at home looks like!

Have a great evening, everyone.

Grandpa

22nd December 2015

Caption: No, I don't know how they got here either 😂 x

Good evening, all. And so the update… Eating better, sleeping better, laughing more, no temperatures, no infections! It would appear our little hero is doin' pretty damn good! Honestly, everyone, it's amazing to see her like this. Not a care in the world, just having fun and family time. It makes you realise just how much we take for granted. Go grab hold of your sons, daughters, grandchildren, nieces, and nephews and give them a hug and watch them smile. It's a gift from the gods 😊

Sorrelle has a day trip to hospital tomorrow to check her levels and have any top-ups she needs. They will then let her out for Christmas. We will let you know how that went in tomorrow's post.

Take care, all.

Grandpa

23rd December 2015

Caption: Hey, Jacob. How about you and me – Bonnie & Clyde? Just saying 😊 x

Good afternoon, everyone. As promised, an update following Sorrelle's visit to the hospital. Her counts are all stable and no blood or platelets were needed, so that's the first big tick. Then a chat with the nutrition team – a little bit of weight loss but nothing to worry them. They are happy she is eating and that her weight seems proportional to her build and size, so half a tick there. And so to the MRD test result… A question for you all – are you happy with one and a half ticks or would you like a huge gold star?! I'm going for the gold star!

Let me explain. You will all remember an earlier post about the last MRD result measuring 3% – and it being higher than hoped. And so to today's results… How does 0.03 % sound?! 🎉👍🎉👍 As you can imagine, delighted doesn't come close! What this means in simple terms is, she's winning! We will, of course, keep you posted with treatment, but for now her reward is an extra day out of hospital. So, Boxing Day at home, too, and then the fight continues 😊

I don't think there will be too much to tell you over the next few days and so I will do the next post when Sorrelle goes back to hospital on the 27th. I will, however, post our regular caption picture to give you all a smile for the day, especially from Sorrelle.

To all our family and friends, thank you, as ever, for your amazing support. We all send you loving wishes for a very happy and peaceful Christmas.

Grandpa

24th December 2015

Caption: Newsflash! Sorrelle makes a surprise visit to grandpa at work and of course holds court 😊 x

25th December 2015

Caption: So, this chubby guy with a white beard and red coat tells me I can have whatever I want... Looks like I got it 😊 😊 x

26th December 2015

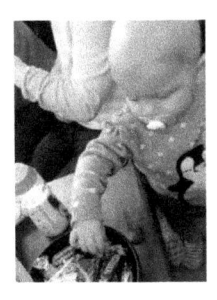

Caption: Hmm, Christmas sweeties. Nobody will notice 😊 x

27th December 2015

Caption: Hey, Grandpa, you're multi-tasking! But you're a man! 😂 x

Good evening, everyone. And so, after what can only be described as a magical Christmas for Sorrelle with her mummy, daddy and family, it's now back to beating the leukaemia! We certainly have it on the run. Our little hero has now safely returned to her second home and the nurses are glad to see her 😊 Numbers have been done, and all is well enough to begin her chemotherapy tonight. Her blood count was just a tiny bit low, so she had a slight top-up of that too.

She's in great spirits and had some lunch with Mummy and Daddy and has been full of smiles and mischief. The break for Gem and Dean has been wonderful and was much needed. Everyone's now refreshed and ready.

As always, I will keep you posted. It remains for me to say I hope you all had a lovely Christmas and to thank you for your warm wishes.

Enjoy the pictures and, as always, caption to follow.

Grandpa

28th December 2015

Caption: Yep, and while you're focusing on my irresistible smile, I'll be pinching the chocolates 😊 This is a baby with brains x

Evening, all. So, the latest on our little hero. First day of chemotherapy went OK. Sorrelle's temp rose to 39.7, and it's knocked her for six. She's done a lot of sleeping. Tonight, her second dose, then next Sunday and Monday will complete this set of treatment. Sounds simple, but obviously there will be temperatures and the odd poorly day. But she is OK, just sleepy and lethargic.

Nothing much else to tell you at this stage. Catch you all tomorrow.

Grandpa

29th December 2015

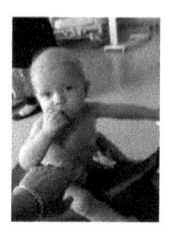

Caption: So, look at these eyes. I'm expecting at least 50 awws 😊 x

Good afternoon, everyone. So, an earlier update today. Off the lines now as no more chemotherapy until next Sunday. Now we wait for the inevitable temperatures and poorliness. We're waiting for her numbers and guessing she'll need a top-up because she looked a little pale and that's usually the sign for needing blood and/or platelets. At the same time, she's happy enough, is drinking well and having the odd nibble of food. As always, they are delighted with her and there are no concerns at all. If we are very lucky, Gem and Dean may get to take her home for a couple of days Thursday or Friday, but that does very much depend on her immune system. We will wait and see.

In the meantime, enjoy the pictures and have a great day.

Grandpa

30th December 2015

Caption: Hey, Mummy, how do you think we'll be doing by next Christmas? We'll be winning, Sweetheart, that's how we'll be doing 😊 x

Good afternoon, everyone. So, today's news. Temperature normal, numbers steady. She had a lumbar puncture today, which is perfectly normal. Just to continue tests and monitoring. Saw our professor earlier, and he's very happy with her progress. He will chat to Gem and Dean tomorrow about the treatment plan for the new year. Other than that, she's sleepy, but that's due to the procedure. Nothing much else to tell you. I have the good fortune to be doing the overnight shift, so I'll have lots of cuddles to tell you about tomorrow.

Have a good evening, all.

Grandpa

31st December 2015

Good afternoon, everyone. Today's caption is also the post for today.

Caption: So, Mummy, we got Christmas at home … how about we have New Year too! 😊

Yes, that's right, folks! They're really happy with Sorrelle's numbers and so they've allowed her to go home for New Year and come back to hospital on Sunday for her next treatment. Last night was really good. She slept for around 10 hours and was full of giggles once the effects of the LP (lumbar puncture) had worn off. 😊 Always cautious when I say this, but things are going well. Obviously, there's a way to go, but this is as good as it gets so far.

To all of you out there following our little munchkin's progress, we wish you a happy, healthy and peaceful new year. May it bring you and your families happiness. Once again, my heartfelt thanks on behalf of Team Sorrelle for all your support, kindness and love.

Enjoy.

Grandpa x

2016

JANUARY 2016

1st January 2016

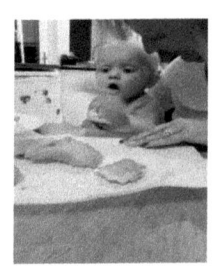

Caption: Hmm, fish and chips – best medicine in the world.

Good evening, everyone. A short update for you, just to let you know that our little hero is very well and enjoying more great time at home. Eating well, smiling lots 😊 Back to the fight on Sunday, when treatment recommences. I'll next update then.

Happy New Year, one and all.

Grandpa

3rd January 2016

Caption: Hey, Dad! Another night at home! 😊

Yep, that's right, everyone, no treatment today. Arrived at hospital ready for treatment, but her platelets were too low and so they will try again tomorrow, possibly after a top-up. Just a case of wait and see. But, hey, an extra night at home is always good news. Will update you tomorrow when we know more.

Have a good evening, everyone.

Grandpa

4th January 2016

Caption: Some girls have motorbikes. Today, I thought I'd try a bouncy zebra 😄

x

Good evening, everyone. Time to return to the daily update. As you can guess, our little hero is once again back on the ward. She's had her next dose of chemotherapy and has another tomorrow, which will complete the third round of treatment. She's doing well – counts are OK, but they will start to fall for a week or two and then begin that recovery again. You regular readers will be familiar with the patterns by now and you may even be getting to be a bit of an expert. It certainly does creep up on you. Prior to 22nd August, I'd never have imagined our family having to be so knowledgeable about leukaemia.

Gem and Dean will get to see the professor tomorrow, and as soon as we know the plans, we'll share the news. Please keep the messages of support coming. They are so very welcome and really do help Gem and Dean.

Have a good evening, everyone.

Grandpa

5th January 2016

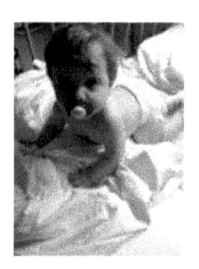

Caption: August 2015 – two years you say, Mummy? Well, I'll have to see what I can do about that!

Good evening, everyone. Apologies for the delay tonight, it's been a long day. And so today's news. Sorrelle's numbers are stable, though a little low, but this is totally normal. And after seeing her tonight, take my word for it, she is totally fine – in great spirits and being as mischievous as ever. Her platelets are a little low and will probably need a top-up in the next day or two. Her last dose of chemotherapy for this round is at 4am tomorrow, and then we wait for the dip before her recovery, which should take four or five weeks. And so what happens next, you may ask? Well, today, we found out the answer to that.

You'll remember at the beginning of this battle us telling you about a two-year process for Sorrelle to become cancer-free, and that there would be side effects, ups and downs, etc. Well, the two-year thing has changed! Her last MRD result showed 0.03% of cancer left… Because this is so low, instead of a two-year chemotherapy treatment plan, Sorrelle will instead receive a bone marrow transplant. This last treatment and a special 10-day course of chemotherapy just before the transplant should finish off the last bit of cancer. Without a transplant, there's a higher risk of relapse. But with a transplant, the chance of relapse is reduced by 65%! This is good news, folks. The timescales are as follows:

4/5-week recovery from this current dose

10 days of high-level chemotherapy

Bone marrow transplant infused – this will be painless (takes about half an hour)

6 weeks of high isolation (to reduce the chance of infection and check her body's accepting the transplant)

And here's the real important bit… Then CANCER-FREE!

RING THE BELL!

Followed by several weeks of monitoring and medication to ensure no rejections.

And then Sorrelle carries on with life, with check-ups of course!

Pretty mind-blowing stuff. Obviously, with any treatment and transplant, there are risks, but we've been here before, and I must stress the professor is VERY happy with how well she is.

One point you'll need to be aware of – if you would like to visit Sorrelle, then it needs to be within the next five weeks. Once she's admitted to the bone marrow ward, they'll only allow the same two nominated people onto the ward. There's no way around this, no matter the circumstances.

We're entering another phase of the unknown, but the medics are confident. To think that by April, Sorrelle could be ringing the cancer-free bell almost has me shedding a tear!

Keep your messages coming and, please, if you have questions, ask them. We will always tell you what we know. I hope this update brings a smile or two and the odd happy tear. We still have a way to go, and there will be ups and downs. But we are so close to the prize, we can almost touch it!

Have a good evening, all. Our little hero is winning!

Grandpa

7th January 2016

Caption: Hey dad you appear to be growing a ginger beard !

Evening, all. And so today's news from planet Sorrelle 😊

Pretty non-eventful day to be honest. Numbers were a little low, as we knew they would be, and so this evening Sorrelle had a top-up of platelets and blood. The third round of chemotherapy has now ended and her immune system is 1.3, which is quite high. That means if she remains stable enough, they could let her home again, with Gem and Dean taking her in for checks every few days. We will have to see how the next day or two go. There's no further treatment scheduled, until the bone marrow transplant in February. The plan now is to recover from round three.

Sorrelle's in high spirits and still doing her fair share of smiling, even with a little sickness tonight. Oh, and her temperature is totally normal. Now this can change in a matter of hours, and it's usually in the first week or two after treatment when the dip occurs. So, we will wait and see and take advantage of her feeling OK and possibly having a little more time at home. As always, we will keep you posted.

Can I just thank you all for your lovely comments after last night's post. I'm truly delighted the posts both comfort you and inform you. It's something I can do to combat the frustration of the things I'd like to do! But that's just a dad and a grandpa thing. Again, my humble thanks.

Have a good evening, everyone.

Grandpa

8th January 2016

Caption: Homeward bound !

Good evening, everyone. So, today's post is a pretty short one. I'll let you guess what the picture means! Yep, that's right, they have let her go home 😊 Back to hospital for check-ups on Monday as there's no more treatment for now. The thinking was, that while her numbers are good, there's no need to be in hospital 😊 Obviously if she gets a bit low, then she'll go back in.

She's polished off a minced beef pie and some fish, which is really important as she's lost a little more weight. The big focus now is for the little munchkin to get some weight on. They checked her numbers before she left hospital, and they're all high. Gem and Dean are delighted to be home. I will once again pause on the posts and keep sending the captions out instead just to keep you up to date pictorially.

Have a great evening, everyone.

Grandpa

9th January 2016

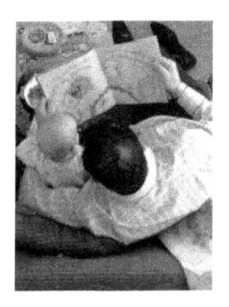

Caption: At home, with Grandpa and stories. What we call a "munchkin's great day".

Good afternoon everyone, nothing to report today other than some quality home time with the little warrior. She is happy and enjoying time with the family and even a little story time with me.

11th January 2016

Caption: Here we go again, Mummy…

Good evening, everyone, and welcome back to the daily hospital posts. Our little hero has been admitted back onto the ward. Time to keep medical tabs on her and help get her numbers up. They had dropped while she was at home, quite a lot really, and so she's had platelets today, for a start. And then we had a spike in temperature to over 38, which, as we all know by now, means antibiotics for at least 48 hours. She's still in great spirits and has taken to feasting on egg mayo sandwiches! We're guessing she'll be a little low for the next week or so, before recovery kicks in. They might let her home prior to the bone marrow transplant. Well, nothing more to share at this point.

Have a good evening, all.

Grandpa

12th January 2016

Caption: Yes, Grandpa, I know you want me to eat it, but would you?!

Evening, everyone. And so this evening's news. Sorrelle slept a little this afternoon and when she woke, she was a bit lethargic and pale, but no temperature to worry about. We think it's the effects of the treatment, and after about an hour, she perked up, as you can see. She's lost a little weight, which you can probably tell from the pictures, and so we think she may need to be tubed tomorrow for feeds. Not ideal, but if it has to be done, then so be it. Still on antibiotics following the spike in temperature yesterday. Other than this, it's onward and upward, continue with count recovery and be ready for the transplant in a few weeks.

Take care, all.

Grandpa

13th January 2016

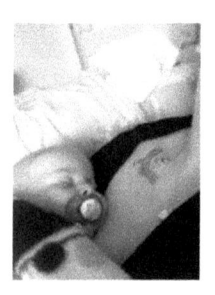

Caption: A tough day today mummy, this girl needs to rest

Good evening, all.

Latest news from the world of Sorrelle… Well, her immune system is pretty low, and she needed a couple of bags of blood today, so this tells us that the latest round of treatment is starting to show itself. Doesn't make for the best of times, but our little hero is doing good. We also have a strange thing going on with her weight – namely that she has put weight on but too much for the timescale, so something isn't quite right. Nothing to worry about, health-wise, it's more likely to be the scales! All in all, she's still smiling, even though she's a little pale.

Grandpa is on Saturday night sleepover duty, which is always fun, so there will be some new pics to keep you all smiling. In the meantime, keep the messages coming. Always good for Gem and Dean to read them, especially in what I would call limbo time.

Have a good evening, all.

Grandpa

14th January 2016

Caption: Arise Sorrelle,

Good evening, all.

Today's news… Platelets low and top-up needed. Looks like our little hero has an infection in her line. She seems OK and her temperature's OK. They're giving her a strong antibiotic to nip anything in the bud nice and quick. Other numbers are OK and not much else to report, other than tomorrow is tube day. On a very positive note, today's caption is a video caption! And it's a belter 😊

Have a good evening, all.

Grandpa (video of Sorrelle walking)

15th January 2016

Caption: Anybody want to break me out? 😊 x

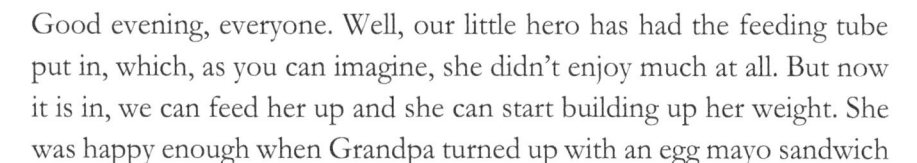

Good evening, everyone. Well, our little hero has had the feeding tube put in, which, as you can imagine, she didn't enjoy much at all. But now it is in, we can feed her up and she can start building up her weight. She was happy enough when Grandpa turned up with an egg mayo sandwich

😊 Temperature is normal, as are her numbers, given the treatment. Immune system pretty low. Bloods and platelets OK, though they will drop again and need a top-up soon. Grandpa is staying over tomorrow, so we have lots of mischief planned 😊

Have a good evening, all, and enjoy the pictures.

Grandpa

16th January 2016

Caption: And the dummy goes there! And I'll put this rubber thing in his mouth too!

Good evening, everyone. And so to the Sorrelle news... As you can see, she's keeping Grandpa busy – and I have to say, it's the best kind of busy there is! She's feeling just fine, and her numbers are all stable as she continues to recover from the last bout of treatment. She's eaten a little bit here and there and has had some feed through the tube. Still a way to go on the eating and weight front, but we will keep you posted on that. Right now, she is OK.

As I write this, she's off into Dreamland, after a biscuit and milk and the obligatory cuddles from Grandpa. Thought you may all enjoy a caption video tonight.

I wish you all a good evening and Gem and Dean a good chill.

Grandpa

17th January 2016

Caption: Eating on the floor grandpa not off the floor 😊

Evening, all. Hope you are all well. Time for an update following my evening with our little hero. Well, it was delightful spending the night with her. She was full of smiles and giggles, had a little to eat and slept from around 9pm, then woke with a lovely smile, had breakfast, then fell asleep on Grandpa, in a chair, until Mummy arrived 😊

We think she may have a bit of mucositis, but it doesn't seem to be causing her any distress. It's one of the normal side effects, and she has had it before, but this time it seems a little milder. The recovery continues the march towards a transplant in February, all being well.

Nothing more to tell at this point. Glad you enjoyed the video caption last night. Think I may treat you all to another from this morning 😊

Have a good evening, all.

Grandpa

18th January 2016

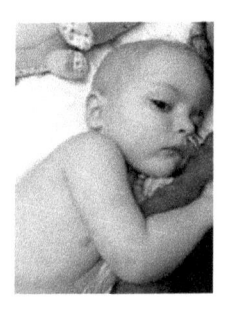

Caption: Not tonight grandpa

Good evening, everyone. Apologies for the late update. As you can see from tonight's pictures, our little hero has had a pretty iffy day. High temperature and heart rate. Please try not to worry – we have seen this before and the medical team have the answers. She's on the right antibiotics and once the cultures come back tomorrow, I'm sure they will make any adjustments to get her over this latest bug. She's warmer than usual and a little sleepy/lethargic but still trying to be happy. Gotta love those eyes, bless her. She had platelets this morning and so, actually, her colour doesn't look too bad. It's part of the roller coaster, and a reminder that our little hero is dealing with some pretty nasty stuff – but we are winning.

Sleep well, everyone.

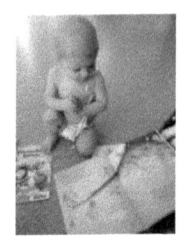

Grandpa

19th January 2016

Caption: It's OK, Dad, use my toy one. I know you can't use the grown-ups' one!

Good evening, everyone. So, our little hero is a bit better today. Her temperature is steady again and her heart rate is back to normal. Two bags of blood, platelets are steady, and the tube feeding is going well, which means she's tolerating the feeds and getting the nutrition she needs. Those eyes are starting to sparkle again, and the smile is almost back to full smile mode 😊 And so we continue the march towards a transplant and hopefully a little time at home before that process begins.

Grandpa

20th January 2016

Caption: Who's the superhero? You decide…

Good evening, everyone. The next update for you. Numbers are not too bad – fluctuating a little but showing signs of stabilising. The infections in her line have been identified, and she's now receiving the correct antibiotics to clear her line. Her temperature hasn't spiked, though. She's tolerating more tube feeds – this is really good news as it means she's getting the calories she needs and she should put some weight on.

Nothing more to tell you, other than you might notice one of today's pictures is outside. Very good reason for this … there were special visitors! The caption will explain everything!

Have a good evening, everyone.

Grandpa

21ˢᵗ January 2016

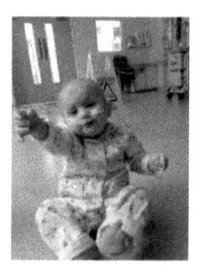

Caption: Can a girl get a hug…

Good evening, all. So, today, the news is pretty good. No weight loss, which is a step in the right direction. Her numbers are all pretty good, and with a little luck, we may even get her home next week. Time will tell, but she really is starting to sparkle again 😊

Still scheduled for transplant some time in February, but first there will be the MRD test to check how much of the disease remains.

Well, not much more to say. Our little hero really is doin' OK.

Have a good evening, all, and enjoy the caption.

Grandpa

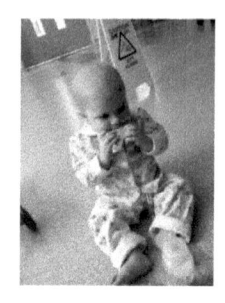

22ⁿᵈ January 2016

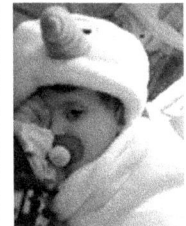

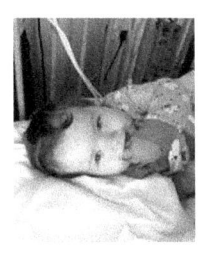

Caption: It's a long journey…

Good evening, everyone. Tonight is the five-month anniversary of Sorrelle's diagnosis. Tonight's pictures are a timely reminder that even at the start of this journey, smiles didn't stop, hopes didn't disappear, dreams didn't fade. It's true that day changed many people's lives, not least our little hero's and her incredibly strong parents'. I think now's a good time to reflect on the last five months. Sorrelle, Dean and Gemma have endured more in this short time than, thankfully, most people will ever have to endure. They've remained strong and positive and although we have supported them, in many ways they've supported us too. I think this is a time to celebrate what we have, as a family and as a group of friends. The last five months have touched us all and reminded us that we are fragile, that the unknown is just that, and to embrace what we have every day.

I want to thank every one of you for the support you continue to show, for the love you share with us, for simply being there, for the money you've raised, for the hope you give, for the dreams you have allowed Dean and Gem to consider, for the way you all care. I've said it many times – your messages do make a difference to Gem and Dean and, in total honesty, they help me too. Seeing my daughter, her partner and my granddaughter being supported by you all touches me deeply. Thank you.

And so the battle continues to the day we ring that bell and know joy like no other.

Have a good evening, everyone.

Grandpa

22nd January 2016

Caption: A father and his princess rest together and dream of the future ♥

23rd January 2016

Caption: Hey, Mummy, are you SURE cousin Eliza wanted to come? She doesn't seem convinced...

24th January 2016

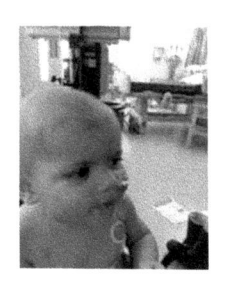

Caption: keep smiling

Good evening, all. So, latest news for today... Pretty much the same as yesterday 😁 Might be a very short update. She's in great spirits. Numbers are nice and stable. It will take spiked temperatures to stop her going home next week – seems all the crossing of everything is working :) And today her weight increased! By very little, but at least it went up. On that basis, they're going to increase the feeds a little, given that she's tolerating them. In the meantime, count recovery continues, as do the smiles, bless her.

Have a good evening.

Grandpa

25th January 2016

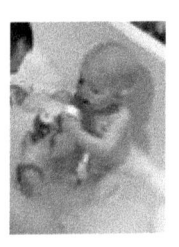

Caption: Nice and clean for home

Good evening from Sorrelle's world. And so today's news… Pack for home! Yep, that's right, our little munchkin got the green light today to go home tomorrow! She'll pop back in every few days for count checks. She has her MRD this week. C'mon, folks, you remember what this is! There'll be a quiz later hahaha. It's the test for Measurable Residual Disease 😊 It's part of the information used to ready her for the transplant and last time, this measured 0.03%. As always, we'll let you know the results when we have them, which should be in around 10 days.

She's in great spirits, as are Mummy and Daddy after hearing they get some home time! Well, not much more to tell you. Like last time, now that Sorrelle will be home, I'll update every couple of days so Gem, Dean and the munchkin have some family time 😊

Enjoy the pictures and caption.

Grandpa

25th January 2016

Caption: Don't drop me now, nursie. I'm outta here tomorrow! 😆

28th/29th January 2016

Caption: Just another day at the office 😊

Evening, everyone. Hope you enjoy the captions tonight. A quick update for you… Sorrelle popped back into hospital today and her counts had got quite low, so she's had blood and platelet top-ups. They're having a look at why they dropped, and we'll know more in the next day or two. It does mean there may be a delay on the transplant, but please don't worry, she's fine in herself. Just need to make sure her counts build well enough before the transplant.

In the meantime, she's happy, if tired, after her checks today, and as you can see from the pictures, she's getting on with things. Just noticed today how lovely her eyelashes are, now they've grown back 😊 Little things we take for granted, eh?

Take care, all.

30th January 2016

Caption: Yes you… get my dinner ready

A very good evening, everyone. As you can see, our little hero is just fine. And for the first time since diagnosis, a very lucky Granny and Grandpa have Sorrelle to stay for the night 😊 Truly amazing. A few medicines to give her, but such a joy to see her laugh, giggle and eat. She's back in hospital for some checks on Monday and so tonight Gem and Dean are having a night off. Sorrelle's numbers are steady once more and, were it not for the tubes, you really would think there was nothing wrong at all. It's strange at times, knowing there is.

Anyway, as promised, a short update to let you know she is very well indeed. The time at home with the little princess is proving to be so precious for Gem and Dean.

Have a great evening, folks. I sure am 😊

Grandpa

FEBRUARY 2016

1st February 2016

Caption: My favourite part of the day ... book rhymes that Mummy doesn't like 😊

Evening, everyone. Well, after a lovely weekend of eating, laughing, sleeping and mischief, it was off to the hospital today for a check on Sorrelle's numbers. The professor is once again delighted with her. Her counts are good, and he has no concerns, which means only one thing – back home! See you Thursday! We reckon that until they're ready to take her in for preparation for the bone marrow transplant she will stay at home and have regular checks at the hospital. As you can imagine, Dean and Gem are enjoying approaching something of a normal family life and making the most of their little munchkin's time at home. I will post an update every few days while she's at home, mainly so I'm not pestering Gem and Dean for news and pictures 😊 Anyway, hope you are all well.

Enjoy your evenings.

Grandpa

4th February 2016

Caption: Wish Mummy would buy me some more toys 😊

Good evening, everyone. So, time for an update. Sorrelle went into hospital today to have her counts checked and the results were as follows: platelets UP, blood UP, temperature PERFECT, immune system UP! In a nutshell, they are delighted with her. She has put on weight, which is wonderful, and she is now back at home having fun with Mummy and Daddy and doesn't need to go back to hospital until next week, when we will have the results of the MRD test. Next week they will give her a dose of chemotherapy, to keep her topped up, and some steroids. We suspect this is all about getting ready for the transplant period and the treatment just before it. We're getting nearer to the day when we can watch her ring that bell.

In the meantime, Gem, Dean and Sorrelle are enjoying a much-needed bout of good-old normal family living 😊 Do feel free to message them if you are in the area. I'm sure if you'd like to visit, you'd be welcome. Do please remember to message them first 😊 Difficult to cope with Sorrelle's fame and fans! Hahaha.

Well, have a great evening, everyone, and I will update again at the weekend, probably on Sunday.

Grandpa

5th February 2016

Caption: A video that just makes you smile ☺

Hi, everyone. I know I said I would send you an update on Sunday but I couldn't resist sending this for you all to see. Our little hero has really found her feet! Makes your heart smile ☺ ☺

As you can see, Sorrelle is really doing well.

(Sorrelle walking confidently for the first time, at home.)

7th February 2016

Caption: Hey, Mummy and Daddy, looks like I'm in the spotlight again ☺

Good morning, everyone. Well, as you can see, the first thing to say is our little hero is doin' pretty good! Actually, very good! Her counts are good, her weight is better. In fact, I haven't seen her look this well since before her diagnosis ☺ So, the pictures you see… Well, last night, a very special lady called Ve decided to arrange a fundraising night for Sorrelle. What seemed like a 200-strong army of wonderful people gave us all a fantastic evening and raised an overwhelming £2,675!

There are no words to adequately convey our family's thanks to everyone who played a part in this night.

I have to say, it's a rather lovely way to start a Sunday morning.

Have a great day, everyone.

Grandpa

10th February 2016

Caption: Yes, Daddy, I'll have a picture with you all, but you're not all getting in here! 😊

Good evening, everyone. As I mentioned at the weekend, Sorrelle is off to hospital in the morning for a check-up and a top-up of chemotherapy, to keep those nasty cancer cells at bay until they decide on dates for the bone marrow transplant. She's been having a wonderful time at home, and her health's been amazing. You can now see from her pictures she's putting on weight, is loving the walking thing, and she had a wonderful evening at her fundraising night 😊

As for the night, it was quite remarkable and very humbling. The way in which everyone pulled together and demonstrated overwhelming generosity was inspirational. For those who missed the weekend post, here's a little update.

These amazing people raised a staggering £2,675 on the night! Disneyland is getting nearer! No words can describe my gratitude. There wasn't a dry eye in the house when the total was announced. A special mention to a very talented young lady who gave us a moving acoustic rendition of *Fight Song*, which, for those of you new to the group, is Sorrelle's song and was actually released in the same week as her diagnosis. There were signed footballs and football shirts, food, cakes, gifts, vouchers – the list goes on. A karaoke with a difference! A wonderful night.

So, to the army of supporters, organisers, donators of prizes, and all of you out there, a huge THANK YOU!

I will post the latest news tomorrow evening following the hospital visit, when we'll hopefully have the results of the MRD test.

Have a good evening, all.

Grandpa

12th February 2016

Caption: Hey, this is the biggest bowl of M&M's I've ever seen 😂

Good evening, everyone. Time for an update on the little hero. Well, first, her numbers are pretty good, and she has put on LOADS of weight! Now answering to Chubby Chops 😊 She's gone back into hospital as her temperature went over 38. So, she's a bit warm, but the same cheeky little thing we all love. The results on the MRD – well, they were a little higher than they wanted and so there's a hold on the transplant. She's going to have another round of chemotherapy next week, hopefully starting Monday but maybe Wednesday.

I will post over the weekend and let you know what happens. For now, she is hot but happy. On with the battle.

Have a good weekend, everyone.

Grandpa

14th February 2016

Caption: Give us a smile then 😊

Good evening, everyone. A quick update for you. Sorrelle's temperature has returned to normal and, as you can see, her smile tells us she's feeling pretty good. Her counts are good, and there are no concerns with her feeding. Probably tomorrow, we'll embark on another round of chemotherapy so we can get this MRD down to where it needs to be in preparation for the bone marrow transplant. Nothing more to tell you at the moment. I will catch up with you all tomorrow night and give you an update on the first day of the treatment round.

Have a good evening, everyone.

Grandpa

15th February 2016

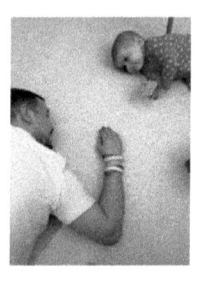

Caption: Dad, are you sure we can hear people in Australia? I think you're telling me porkie pies 😊

Good evening, everyone. A quick update on treatment for Sorrelle today and the coming days. Today she begins another round of chemotherapy so we can get that MRD down. This treatment cycle will run until 2nd

March and will involve treatment every couple of days with one- or two-day gaps in between. The side effects are pretty similar to the ones we've seen before, so no great alarm bells there. And she will also have a course of steroids, which, if you remember, will bulk her up a little. She's had another really good day – and two breakfasts! She's been walking up a storm and has been flat out, resting up. Her numbers are very good and so she's well prepared for this next course of treatment. Please keep those messages of support coming for Gem and Dean. I hope you enjoy tonight's caption picture, which, I have to say, as a father and grandpa, truly warms my heart.

Have a good evening, everyone.

Grandpa

16th February 2016

Caption: More autographs to write, Mum?! Think you and Dad had better do some for me 😆

Good evening, all. Second day of treatment for this round, and Sorrelle is once again handling it with her usual bravery. This treatment seems to be making her very sleepy. I'll be honest – we'll take that every time! She's a little wobbly on her feet, but there don't seem to be any of the horrible side effects we associate with chemotherapy. Her weight is now officially back on track for her age and size. As for numbers today, all good, no top-ups needed. She will probably need some in the weeks ahead, but for now she is really pretty good.

Hope you have a good evening.

Grandpa

19th February 2016

Caption: Another one of those pictures that simply doesn't need a caption 😊

Good evening, everyone. Update time. Well, firstly, our little hero is home 😊 Her numbers are very good. Platelets over 200, immune system 5.6, red blood over 100! She's almost a week into this round of treatment, and she's coping with it really well. She's in a little discomfort, which shows in her being a little quieter than normal and not toddling around as much. Thankfully, there don't seem to be any of the more unpleasant side effects. She's attending hospital every day for medication, which only takes 20 minutes, and then home again. The next chemotherapy drug is on Monday and so Grandpa gets a little visitor tomorrow night. There will be a Grandpa breakfast ready for her on Sunday morning 😊

Enjoy your evenings, everyone.

Grandpa

23rd February 2016

Good evening, everyone. Time for an update on how our little hero's doing. The first thing to say is she's really well. Her immune system's measuring 2.5, her platelets 180 and red count 105. These are all really positive numbers, and explain why she looks so good. Her colour and her weight are all good too. You will remember how much importance I've placed on her eating and gaining weight. So far, this stands her in good stead.

Today, Sorrelle went onto the ward for her next chemotherapy, and they were so pleased with how she is that they sent her back home for more quality time with Gemma and Dean. She will receive her next dose on Thursday, on the day case ward. I am sure they'd be happy to see anyone who'd like to pop round, so long as you make arrangements with them first.

Next week, Rob (Professor Wynn) will do the MRD test, and we will wait and see if this treatment has reduced the MRD, as we move towards the transplant.

You'll see from the caption video that the little munchkin stayed with us on Saturday night. What you are watching is a lovely Sunday morning just after breakfast with Grandpa 😊 Precious moments.

Well, nothing much more to tell you. I will update on Thursday after the next chemotherapy. Have a good evening, all, and enjoy the video, complete with toddling and smiles 😊

Grandpa

26th February 2016

Caption: You sure there are real bears in here, Mummy? 😊

Good morning, all. Time for a Sorrelle update. As you can see from the picture, ole Chubby Chops is back haha. She's eating pretty well and, importantly, she's putting on weight. All part of being ready for her transplant and the intense chemotherapy that comes with it. Her counts are very good and seem to be staying high despite treatment. Next week is the MRD test, the results of which we should get back the following week. They will then schedule the bone marrow transplant for around mid-March. Once the dates have been confirmed, we will, of course, let you know. For now, we simply enjoy the smiles, the being at home and prepare for what will be a pretty tough couple of months. The prize at the end, God willing, will be more than worth it. It's natural to be nervous as we get nearer to this – and waiting for the MRD – but it's very important we remember the medics have seen this before and that our little hero is in the very best hands. So, try not to worry, keep the messages of support for Gem and Dean coming, and whatever you use for luck, use it. 😊

Have a good day.

Grandpa

MARCH 2016

2nd March 2016

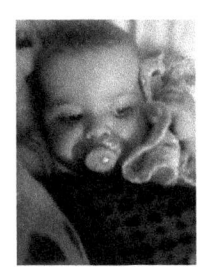

Caption: A long day for a cute hero…

Evening, everyone. Time for an update. OK, so firstly, Sorrelle's numbers. They're all high, and there are no issues at all. She has chemotherapy tomorrow, and then this cycle ends. Today was the MRD test, and we'll know the results next Thursday. It will be yet another anxious time waiting to see if this round has reduced her MRD and whether she is ready for her bone marrow transplant in the next few weeks. Generally, she is really well, but not today. Today, she's been poked and prodded, put under, etc., so she's tired. She'll be fine tomorrow, though. She really has been very happy and eating like crazy and she's put on weight.

I will do another update at the weekend, when there will be more smiles from our little hero. Now is the time for a message or two for Gem and Dean. That would be a big help. Do what you can, everyone.

Take care.

Grandpa

5th March 2016

Caption: It's official. I love my cousin 😊

Good evening, everyone. And so here we are following another round of treatment. Now we wait for the next MRD result, which is due next Thursday. The waiting is never easy. All we can do in the meantime is enjoy the days. As you can see, Sorrelle is really well and spending some wonderful quality time with family and friends. Her counts are all good, and there's no need to go back to hospital before the results next Thursday.

Keep everything crossed, everyone. We will update you as soon as we know.

Have a good evening.

Grandpa

9th March 2016

Caption: How does that song go again? I remember now... "I'm the king of the swingers" 😊

Hello, everyone. Thought I would send a quick update while we ready ourselves for tomorrow. I wanted to share with you all how well Sorrelle has been these past couple of weeks. It really is baffling when you see her to know she is so poorly. The caption picture was taken a couple of days ago. She's doing all the things a perfectly well child would be doing. She came over for a few hours last night and she didn't stop giggling, walking, smiling and eating until home time! This grandparent stuff is pretty damn good – I might just take to it!

And so to tomorrow. I suspect there will be a few late nights, a few nails being bitten, some pacing, and a few fingers being crossed. Tonight will be a long night for Gem and Dean, and tomorrow will, I am sure, be filled with apprehension. We're hoping to have the results sometime after lunch, so we'll let you know as soon as we can where we're at.

If ever there was a night you fancied dropping a message to Gem and Dean, tonight's the night, folks. Keep positive, try not to worry, and I'll be back tomorrow with the latest news.

Have a good evening, everyone.

Grandpa

10th March 2016

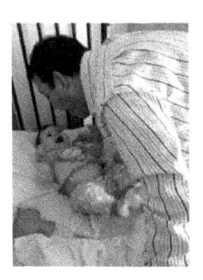

Caption: Hey, Grandpa. Here we are in August 2015. You never know, things may be better by March 2016 😊 The 10th to be precise!

Good afternoon, everyone. So, here we are. Finally, the MRD results. We all know the roller coaster of the last MRD reading at 0.9%. This figure is important – at nearly 1%.

So, today – the news we all hoped for, wished for, prayed for. How does 0.05% look! Yes, that's right, folks, a big reduction! And here's the most important part – again, something we've all hoped for – we still have a way to go, and a bone marrow transplant, but to put this into context, let me share with you what Sorrelle's professor said today when explaining the results to Gem and Dean: "Now we transplant to cure"! The key word here is cure! This is where we are. By the time Olivia joins us, Sorrelle will be past her treatment – the most memorable words I think I have ever heard.

As for what's next, the transplant will be on Dean's birthday! Chemotherapy on 21st March in preparation for the actual transplant. So, another week at home to enjoy family time. Her numbers, by the way, are excellent and of no concern at all to the medics.

As you can imagine, there has been a lot of very happy emotion today. It's worth pausing to remind ourselves there are still some steps left on the journey and to once again thank the remarkable nurses, doctors, consultants and professors – they're heaven sent! Finally, to thank you, our army of friends and family, who have provided support, love and kindness to Gem, Dean and Sorrelle. I will never be able to thank you enough. All I ever needed was to know Sorrelle would receive the best treatment and Gemma and Dean would have support.

So, now, please share the news. Shout from the rooftops! Laugh, cry, celebrate! We are so close. The bell waits … the end is in sight.

The small boat nearer to the shore in that big ocean!

16th March 2016

Caption: A week in the life of a hero 😉

Good evening, everyone. So, here we are, a few days from the next round of treatment for our little hero. She has been free from hospital for a lovely chunk of time now, and as you can see from the pictures, she is full of smiles and mischief. She is eating really well, and her counts are good. Her colour is back and, unlike before, she isn't getting run down prior to needing bloods. The news last week was amazing, and we are moving forward with determination and hope for a bright future. Of course, there will be a couple of months of very intensive treatment, and I am sure some of those yucky symptoms will return, but we keep focused on the prize and ringing that bell in a matter of weeks. We have come a very long way, and every day Sorrelle continues to be an inspiration to us all. She goes into hospital on Monday (Dean's birthday). I will give you an update on Monday night and let you know when she has settled into the bone marrow ward.

Please, if you get a chance, keep those messages of support coming to Gemma and Dean. Now, more than ever, they mean so much. My focus in doing these updates is to inform you all and to give Gem and Dean the reassurance that we are all thinking of them. You are all making such a difference and believe me when I say that your words and love play an equal part in this journey. Thank you for being the very special people you all are.

Have a great evening.

Grandpa

18th March 2016

Caption: pretzels for supper and scrambled egg for breakfast. Thanks, Grandpa.

20th March 2016

Hey, Dad, I've seen this great toy shelving system for my bedroom. Let's get online and find it. (Take that HOW MUCH?! look off your face – I'm worth it!) Right, c'mon, in my car, let's go collect it!

22nd March 2016

Caption: Who loves ya, Chubby Chops? As Sorrelle said to Daddy!

Good evening, everyone, and welcome to day 1 of the last leg. This picture was taken earlier today, and so I guess you could say our little hero is taking this in her stride, as she has done throughout!

In honesty, the biggest deal is getting back into the routine of hospital after such a lovely break away from it. Of course, the thing we hang onto is this last stretch! Six to eight weeks, and then the bell. And the actual treatment is only two weeks – the rest is recovery.

So how are the numbers today? What happened? Well, she had her first treatment at 10am today, followed by a few blood tests, just to check they have the dosage right for her. Now that's been done, they shouldn't need to do it again. You all know how our little hero likes to throw us the odd curve… Yep, you guessed it – in her own room yesterday for less than an hour and she spikes a 38+ temp! Hahaha bless her. Chances are there's an infection in her line, but as you will have read countless times before, this is all normal stuff and fully to be expected. Temp is now back to normal! Think it was Sorrelle's way of saying "I'm back!" Hahaha.

As for the rest, bloods are OK and immune system is still over 3, even though it's dropped from 5. To put this into context, by the time we get to transplant day, it will be zero, which is what they would expect given treatment. Transplant day is 31st March, we believe – and what they call day zero. It's what Grandpa calls the first day of the rest of her life!

I will post a few more pictures from today so you can all see she's totally fine. Yes, there are gonna be times when she feels pretty low, but, hey, let's enjoy what we can. And please remember how well she has taken to all her treatment and how amazed the medics are with her.

Have a lovely evening, everyone, and I'll catch you all tomorrow.

Grandpa

24th March 2016

Caption: No wheels, no steering wheel, no flashing lights – yep, that's right, it's a box!

Good morning, everyone. Here's the latest update on Sorrelle. We've now had two full days of treatment and, as we expected, it's starting to have an impact on our little hero. The chemotherapy is lowering her counts, and she had some red blood last night. She's also having a drug that lowers her immune system and which gave her a rash for a couple of hours. It's a normal side effect and the rash has now gone. Each day she has this, her body will tolerate it more and the effects will reduce. It has meant that her immune system is now below 1.0, which, again, is expected. One result of all the fluid she has been having is that she has put on weight. However, they give her medication to get rid of this so she doesn't bloat.

She had temperatures of over 38 and over 39 yesterday and has been a little under the weather. This doesn't mean they're concerned about her – they're very happy with how she's coping. And there were a couple of occasions yesterday, where there were a few giggles and quavers! Of course, that doesn't mean she's laughing all day and there are no bad effects. We all know there are going to be effects – otherwise the treatment wouldn't be doing what it needs to be.

So, today's picture is from Monday, only because at the point we thought about a picture yesterday, she was looking a bit red, bless her. I FaceTimed her yesterday and she looked really good and was laughing at me until her penguin movie became more interesting than Grandpa! As if that could happen hahaha.

Well, two days gone, and we get nearer to the 31st and the transplant! Her chemotherapy finishes on the 29th, then the 30th is a rest day. One final point, just to reassure you all – the actual transplant takes around 30 minutes and is just like her having a bag of blood. It's painless. The significance of the transplant is her body accepting it and starting to make good cells rather than bad.

All in all, she's doin' OK and, as always, she's showing us the meaning of bravery and inspiration.

Have a good day, everyone.

Grandpa

25th March 2016

Caption: And there's always the "sleep through it" option 😊

Good morning, everyone. So, here we are on day 4 on the bone marrow ward. Gem and Dean are getting used to life back in the bubble, the doctors and nurses are in their routine, and Sorrelle would rather let us all get on with it and not disturb her! 😊 The first three days of treatment are going exactly to plan. Our little hero's body is behaving and there are no concerns. Does this mean she's not feeling a little ropey? Of course not. But Sorrelle has astounding powers of tolerance and recovery. I'm certain, were it me, I wouldn't cope half as well. Not only does she continue to inspire us all but she teaches us the odd lesson too!

So, the plan today is more of the same, and her last day of treatment prior to transplant will be 29th March. Think of it this way – since the transplant doesn't hurt, the 29th will be the last time they have to put any of that horrible poison in her body! Of course, it's *good* poison, and the very thought that seven months on we would be saying this is the last time is amazing. Her counts are all OK and it's all about levels, almost as though someone in an office is tweaking some kind of medical graphic equaliser switch. (Good analogy there for Great Uncle Dan!)

As you can imagine, there will be no shortage of chocolate on the ward over the weekend! I have a feeling – and hope – our little munchkin will trough her way through lots!

Please do send in your messages of support, especially now. The ward is very isolating, and the room even has serving hatches to minimise contact! Gem and Dean will feel more isolated than ever. And so whilst we can't wave a magic wand and cure Sorrelle, we know what we *can* do.

Every time you send a message and Gem and Dean hear that little ping, it reminds them we care. And, believe me, when they read them, the comforting smile that follows is more of a medicine than you can imagine.

Thank you once again for being an army of comfort.

Grandpa

27th March 2016

Caption: I know it's pasta, Dad, but I'm eating it 'cos it looks like wiggly worms 😊

Good morning, everyone. Only three days of treatment left! And another day nearer to ringing the bell. Our little hero had some visitors yesterday, to make the most of fun time before the isolation begins on transplant day. Sorrelle is more tired now, and having aches and pains, but the medical team anticipated this and they have a suite of pain relief ready to minimise any discomfort. We have been told that one week prior to transplant and the first week post transplant are the worst, and so we roll up our sleeves, keep moving forward and chalk off another day. Sorrelle's counts are all where they need to be. Other counts like potassium fluctuate, but imagine someone behind the scenes constantly adjusting medication to keep Sorrelle just where she needs to be – it's quite a balancing act. Sorrelle tries to be OK. Some hours are better than others, but in the grand scheme of things, she is doing really well.

Gem and Dean are in the zone and getting a little nervous, which is only to be expected. I know I keep saying how remarkable Sorrelle has been through this, but I have to say Gem and Dean find levels of reserve, determination and love that there must be an award for!

And so a Happy Easter to you all. Enjoy your day, eat lots of chocolate, and listen out for that faint sound of the bell. Closer and closer, folks!

Grandpa

28th March 2016

Caption: Damn it, you caught me again 😊

Good evening, everyone. A very short post this evening, just to update you that Sorrelle has had a great day. She really is surprising everyone with how well she is coping with the last of the treatment prior to transplant. Her numbers are pretty good. I'd say she may need platelets and red blood in the next day or two.

I'm saving the longer post for tomorrow evening. A very special post indeed!

Have a good evening, everyone.

Grandpa

29th March 2016

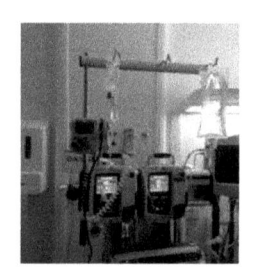

Caption: A special day.

Good evening, everyone. As promised, welcome to a very special update today. There's no picture of Sorrelle, not because she is unwell – actually, she is in great spirits – and not because she is not smiling. Truth is she's been smiling most of the day.

No, our dear family and friends, there is real meaning behind today's picture. I'd like to draw your attention to the suspended bag on the left, which contains something called Melphalan, a chemotherapy drug. To be precise, earlier today, it was the final bag of chemotherapy drug that will ever be given to Sorrelle! This is such a milestone!

Of course, there is the transplant on Thursday and medication along the way, and I am sure she will need platelets and red blood, but to know we are at the end of chemotherapy signals the beginning of a new era for Sorrelle. We have to be sure the transplant works, of course, but there is nothing to suggest it won't and, as a result, we move nearer to the day we can declare her cancer-free. Sorrelle, Gemma and Dean have been on a journey no one should have to endure, and they have done so with determination, grace, resilience, courage and humility worthy of our admiration and respect. Speaking as a father and a grandpa, I have a pride in them that is hard to explain. And I feel a gratitude to the medical teams and to all of you that I will never be able to put into adequate words. This is a very emotional day, for all the best reasons. Through the dark days, the long hospital nights, the isolation, the treatments, the sad news of other little ones who were not so fortunate, the worry, the tears, the frustrations – one thing you hold onto is the hope an innocent child gets a chance, and that a mother and father get to experience all those happy days we take for granted as we watch our children grow. That they look forward to a future of shared moments.

The amazing team on Ward 84 and the bone marrow ward have given those things to Gemma and Dean. Those things we wondered if we'd ever experience last August, are now within reach, and so to all of you out, there a special plea from me – tonight, hold someone close to you, call them, email them, do something to remind them how loved they are. Remember life is fragile and smile to yourself at the wonder of your families and your friends.

Tomorrow is a rest day for Sorrelle. Her new bone marrow will be taken from the donor and will be ready for our little hero on Thursday. I can then update you on the first day of Sorrelle's new future. There will be days ahead where she will need to recover, and maybe feel a little low, but, for now, for today, let's wipe away the tears of joy, take a deep sigh of relief, smile and enjoy our evenings.

Take care, everyone.

Grandpa

31st March 2016

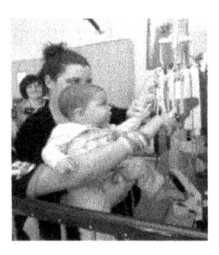

Caption: Taking back my life.

Good afternoon, everyone. So, today's update. At 3:20pm this afternoon, Sorrelle pressed the button that began her bone marrow transplant. Today is the first day of the rest of her life 😊 Let me reassure you all that she's in great shape, she's been eating and laughing all afternoon, and the transplant's not causing her any pain at all. Her numbers are good – blood 80, platelets 20, immune system 1.47 – so later today she will have some platelets. Other than that, no concerns at all. You may see in the picture she looks like she's getting a tan. This is a side effect of the chemotherapy. All perfectly normal. The nurses have just done her obs, and all is fine.

We have now started the strict isolation period for up to three weeks. It'll then be a little more relaxed. However, for the next six months, being careful are the watchwords.

Emotionally, as you can imagine, today is huge. The medics are our heroes; the donor, our guardian angel; and my granddaughter, at such a tender age, probably the most inspirational person I will ever know.

And so we, as a family, our extended family and our dear friends, we all begin the next chapter of this journey – the journey that brings with it recovery, hope, dreams and happiness.

I will continue to give you regular updates during her recovery, up to the time when Sorrelle rings the bell.

Thank you to everyone out there for your continued love, support and messages of encouragement.

Finally, to Gemma and Dean – my respect, love and admiration to you both, not only for the people you are but for the people you have become on this journey. Be under no illusion you both are the reason Sorrelle is here and beating this.

Have a wonderful evening, everyone.

Grandpa

APRIL 2016

1st April 2016

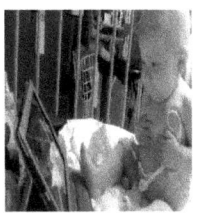

Caption: Tried sleeping through it. Let's try dancing through it 😊 Thanks Great Uncle Dan! Brothers in arms for Sorrelle

(Dancing to Great Uncle Dan's video.)

Good evening, everyone. Well, I am one lucky grandpa tonight 😊 I'm on hospital sleepover! So, I have the evening and the morning in the company of our little hero. As I write this post, she is fast asleep, after watching Snow White and pretty much laughing her way through the day. Great Uncle Dan popped in and Sorrelle was able to show him her dance to his new Christmas single to support Bury Hospice. Thank you Dan for cheering Sorrelle up as she watched the video and became your number one fan! A good point to say thank you to my little brother for being there for me too, I love you kid. As for her numbers, all perfectly OK. She is having some red blood a little later, but other than that we continue to wait for her to drop a little. And still she confounds us by doing what we are starting to call "a Sorrelle"! Basically, doing the opposite of what they expect!

I'm hoping for some cuddles later. I've just introduced her to the Eskimo kiss today and she loves it! She really does do cute quite well! As for Gem and Dean, they are having a well-deserved night off and chilling together at home.

I thought you might all enjoy a caption video tonight, taken earlier today. It's all the evidence you need that Sorrelle is in great shape and is well on the way to recovery. We may still have some down days, but as I've said before, let's take what we can get.

Have a great evening, everyone. I guarantee you I will 😊

On a personal note, can I thank you for your kind words regarding my updates. I'm glad they keep you informed and are of comfort. It is the little something I can do to help us all on this journey. As always, my motive simply remains to provide Gem and Dean with a means of seeing the endless love and kindness you show them every day. So, again, thank you all.

Grandpa

2nd April 2016

Caption: My Friday night with Grandpa and Saturday morning silly time.

Good morning, everyone. So, last night Sorrelle was a joy, and she slept until 8:30 this morning. We laughed, had breakfast, Facetimed Mummy, watched Snow White and now she's drifted off for a nap.

They gave her blood last night, and all other counts are really good. Still we wait for the not-so-good days!

By the way, for any Friday night revellers out there, I'm making a bet my Friday night was better than yours 😊

I'll share the good morning video we did for Gem this morning. Believe me, it'll start your day with a smile 😊

Have a great weekend, everyone.

Grandpa

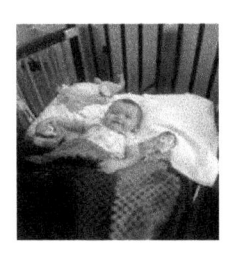

Caption: You can't keep me down for long 😊

Good evening, everyone. First, before I update you on our little hero, can I thank you all for yesterday's messages to Gem and Dean. It was a pretty tough day and night, there was little sleep, and there were a few tears. Your words of support and love really made a difference, so a very personal thank you from me. You did good, folks.

Now on to today. Well, a better day today. They increased Sorrelle's morphine overnight – too much, as it started to have a couple of adverse side effects. Nothing serious, but once they reduced it, she was much better. We know she has a bug, which is spiking her temperature, and she's feeling a little low, but there's been an improvement since yesterday. The mucositis is mild, and although she is sore, she is taking things to her mouth and trying to eat. Her counts are 0 for immune and white cells, but a zero white cell count at this stage is perfect. The reason is that her cancer is generated through her white cells, so it kinda works like this – kill all the white cells … cancer zero … new bone marrow … new white cells from new bone marrow … cancer-free. Obviously, there are other factors but that's the basics. So, what they have done is pretty much press a metaphoric reset button!

My guess is around another week at this level, and then we should see her starting to build her counts on her own without as much need for top-ups. We should see her sores reduce and go, and basically, we should start to see a mini Gemma on the loose! And that, folks, is a worrying thought! Ask Dean – I'm sure he'll concur!

In summary, we're hangin' tough and, more importantly, so is our little hero. She continues to inspire us all and, even at her lowest, she has nurses falling in love with her at every turn! We're not quite out of the woods yet, but the trees are thinning!

Thanks again for all your love and support, our special army out there.

Have a good evening.

Grandpa

7th April 2016

Caption: I'm not reading your newspaper for you as well, Daddy 😊

Good morning, everyone. So, news today on our little hero. Well, we are now one week after transplant and so far, no rejection, which is great. The mucositis is still there but since last night, it seems to be breaking up and so she's a bit more settled. She even had a smile or two and a couple of sips of juice. I reckon another two or three days and that improvement should be much greater.

As for her numbers, her immune system moved from 0 to 0.02, but hey, it's up! She had blood and platelets last night, which will hopefully help her feel better today. Certainly much better than a couple of days ago. And so the recovery continues. A couple of weeks of strict isolation and then we will let you all know about visits.

Have a good day, all.

Grandpa

8th April 2016

Caption: I'll be bouncing around soon, everyone.

Good morning, all. Welcome to the Sorrelle news. The doctors and nurses are really happy with the progress she is making. This is a picture from yesterday. You can clearly see she's not ready for a marathon, but all things are relative and she is only one week post transplant and three weeks post chemotherapy – and this chemotherapy was incredibly strong and both drugs were completely new to her. We were told she would lose her hair and have mucositis again and that this would pretty much floor her. But Sorrelle's power of recovery and her ability to cope with this treatment has surprised everyone. So, in reality, we are somewhere in the middle.

So what does "floor her" mean medically? Well, she has a virus, which she's on antibiotics for, and her oxygen levels are dipping slightly and so the mask you see next to her is to give her a gentle top-up. The mucositis is stopping her eating, and she is a little sore, but this is starting to break up and there are signs it's reducing. And yes, we've had a tear or two. Basically, the little munchkin is feeling a little grotty and doesn't know what to do with herself.

However, two important things. Some of her counts are just starting to bottom out and rise, and I reckon by the end of the weekend she will be in much better spirits. I asked a nurse yesterday – 'cos they're the ones giving the hands-on day-to-day care – how our little hero is doing compared to what they've seen over the years. The answer – apart from loving her to bits – is she's doing better than most children they see!

This is the one to remember, folks. We all know it's a long road, with many ups and downs. Truth is, our downs haven't been as bad as they could have been or like what we've seen on the wards. Our little hero is doin' good. Gem and Dean could do with a damn good rest after it all, that's for sure, but hey there will be time for that … when Sorrelle is 18! All us older parents out there sure know that one!

So, a final rally call as we move towards complete recovery. Keep smiling, keep strong, keep perspective and let's remind ourselves that we *can* endure, no matter how much it might seem we can't.

Have a good day, everyone.

Grandpa

9th April 2016

Caption: Are you sure it doesn't come off, Mummy? 😊

Good morning, everyone. OK, so news on our little hero. Well, there's not much to say to be honest. We're still waiting for white cells and her immune system to arrive, which will show us that the transplant has started to map into her body – that the new bone marrow is producing Sorrelle's counts. In the meantime, the mucositis continues to break down. Maybe by Sunday or Monday, she will feel more like putting food and drink to her mouth. She's ratting a bit with it all breaking down but she's OK. Lots of sleeping mixed with the odd glimpse of mischief. The main thing is to keep her wrapped in cotton wool and keep infections away while her body recovers. It seems like an endless wait, but that's the nature of it.

Have a good weekend, all.

Grandpa

10th April 2016

Caption: Hey, Mummy, you're on TV 😄

Good afternoon, everyone. And so today's update. Well, better than yesterday would be the best description! We have smiles!

Here's a riddle for you. How does a millimetre of chocolate make a grown man cry? Here's how… For the last nine days, Sorrelle's throat has been sore with mucositis. She's not said anything and has kept her mouth closed because it's been so sore. So, today, Grandpa plays a silly game with an Easter egg, just to see if our little hero will smile. We end up with chocolate all over Grandpa, over toys, over our hands … and then it happens. I break off a millimetre, praying she will put it to her lips and the taste will help, and then she takes the tiny piece of chocolate and eats it and smiles. Well, that's Grandpa in tears! This sums up where we are. She's getting there. Her counts are stable, and we wait for them to rise. She still has viruses to get rid of, but each day is a little better and today was a big step. Simply wanting to use her mouth is wonderful progression.

I'll send you some more pictures from this morning.

Have a great day, everyone.

Grandpa

12th April 2016

Caption: Transplant day +12 and smiles.

Good morning, everyone, and welcome to the latest Sorrelle news. As you can see from the picture, things are improving. After a pretty rough week or so, the side effects of the high-dose chemotherapy are starting to diminish. Her hair, as you can see, is getting patchy but, hey, she's about the prettiest little girl I've seen with no hair. And it'll grow back. To think at the start of the journey, it's one of the things you dread, and now it doesn't even register. As for her counts, well, the two important ones now are her white cells and her immune system. The white cells are just starting to appear and within the next couple of days we should see her immune system begin (the new bone marrow generating). As for her virus, she's still on antibiotics, and we get results on this regularly. She's started to mumble words, which is a great sign that her throat is ridding itself of the mucositis. And they have reduced her morphine, which she will soon be off, maybe by the end of today. The professor saw her yesterday and commented on how happy he is with her progress.

So, we carry on the recovery and get ready for the all-important test maybe in a week or two, which will tell us the results of the transplant and the chemotherapy.

It's been a very emotional roller coaster. If you've ever been on one, you'll know that feeling of relief as you're turning the last corner, after the dip, and the station's in sight. We now wait for it to stop and for that bar to be lifted from our knees 😊

Have a great day, everyone.

Grandpa

13th April 2016

Caption: Smile is on its way back 😊

Transplant +13

Good evening, everyone. And so this evening's update. We have white cells, are still waiting for her immune system, and blood and platelets are being topped up, so the breaking news is ... no change 😊 Her professor had a look at her numbers and he is happy that things are improving – just slowly. She's having food through her tube and although she has some sickness, at least with something in her stomach, it isn't causing pain, which it was when she had nothing in her stomach.

So, we're in a period where news is slow. The main thing is her professor is happy. She's smiling a little more now and is dancing to Heigh-Ho, which, by the way, is driving Gemma insane 😊 So, I am sure you will all want to send messages of support ... *to Sorrelle*, to carry on dancing to Heigh-Ho, Heigh-Ho 😄

Have a good evening, everyone.

Grandpa

14th April 2016

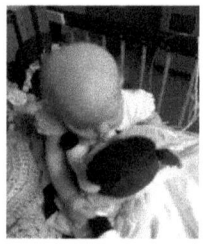

Caption: A very special thank you.

Good evening, everyone, and welcome to the latest update on Sorrelle. We're still waiting for her counts to rise and for her sickness to subside – basically, we're waiting for the end of the mucositis. She's achy, so she's back on the morphine. But then something changed her mood – she had a special delivery all the way from America 😊 Sorrelle's great-great aunt Mini sent a special gift to cheer our little hero up. And, believe me, folks, it did the trick. She hasn't put it down. From a very happy Sorrelle, thank you so much and from all of us, thank you for making her day a little easier. We are sending you lots of love xx

As much as I'd love to tell you more, the truth is we're in a bit of a lull. She continues to soldier on, but as Dean is unwell and can't come in the room, the four walls do seem to be closing in for Gem. And the frustration is palpable for Dean. I've even heard Gem say she's missing him! See, we can still giggle 😊

I'll update again in the next couple of days. Keep those messages of support coming and have a good evening.

Grandpa

16th April 2016

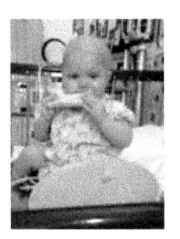

Caption: Hmm, I remember this 😊

Good morning, all. And so the latest news on our little hero. Well, yesterday wasn't a great day. She picked up another virus and had a temp of 39.7 and the shakes. Once the antibiotics and the paracetamol kicked in, she was comfortable, and later in the evening she was smiling and content. Thankfully, the virus was from her line and not from the adenovirus. They are treating this whilst we wait for the new immune system and white cells to come through. The professor can see signs under the microscope – we just need them to push through. Maybe things are just moving a little more slowly. Maybe the chemotherapy has taken longer to work through this time. There could be a number of reasons, but, as we all know, this is a roller coaster. It's a long journey, and Sorrelle has a way of confounding them, which, frankly, we all find pretty frustrating. You think, why can't she be normal? And then you remember who her mum and dad are! Hahaha. And Sorrelle should never be normal because there's simply no such thing.

So on to this morning. Movement in the right direction. She slept for 12 hours, which must have been such a relief for her little body and, of course, for Gem, who needs to sleep too. It's just as important. (You listening, Gem? 😊) This picture was taken about an hour ago – yes, she's trying to eat! Really good sign. I cannot convey just how much this little girl is battling. I've honestly never seen anything like it. No matter how many times she feels down, no matter how many medicines, tubes, prodding, poking, temperatures, side effects – she dusts herself off and simply says OK, what's next! Truly remarkable.

You can see Gem and Dean moving from inspiration to despair on a daily basis. They too are showing a determination and a love that is testament to the people and parents they are. The professor and his team continue to monitor and tinker, and we all wait for the counts to rise. In honesty, folks, it's a waiting game.

Have a good weekend.

Grandpa

17th April 2016

Caption: Tunnel to freedom, Grandpa. I knew this isolation hutch would be useful 😊

Good evening, all. So, Sunday's update. Well, frustrating about sums it up. Laughter, smiles and mischief versus still no counts coming through. The mucositis is working its way out of her system, and she's spiking temperatures. As I've said, it looks like her counts are there under the microscope, it's just a waiting game for them to show on the wider blood tests. They really do think it will be any day. When you spend time with her, it's hard to see how they haven't arrived yet. All in all, she's well, the tests are good, and they're still giving her the medication for the adenovirus. We get the latest results for this on Tuesday. The professor has said that their rate has slowed, so we seem to be moving in the right direction, even if it is so slow! I wish I could tell you more, but it's the nature of science and anatomy. What I can assure you is that she has had the best two days so far – she's smiling and she's had two full nights' sleep the last two nights. I have a feeling when this is all done, they will call it the "Sorrelle Way", a new form of recovery which, trust me, hasn't been seen before. She has more curveballs than the Yankees!

Please try not to worry. She's in the best place with the best professor and a pretty special mummy and daddy. I will update again on Tuesday following the latest test results. If we get the counts through before then, I'll be straight on with the update.

Take care, all.

Grandpa

19th April 2016

Caption: Try not to worry. The smile is getting bigger and the glint in her eye is almost there 😊

Good evening, everyone. I've just returned from yet another audience with HRH Sorrelle 😊 How is she in herself? Pretty good really. Her smile is back, as is the Sorrelle gaze that we last saw a month ago. She's getting a little stronger and once again proving that medicine and Sorrelle is a whole new art, which critics will take a lifetime to understand, let alone poor Professor Wynn! They're happy with her weight, and today they popped a tube back in her nose to start feeds again. The mucositis is still coming out but getting clearer and clearer all the time. She isn't as sore or tired.

So, what about medically? Well, yesterday, she had more blood and platelets and is continuing to have the medication to fight the adenovirus. Some news on this virus – it's finally reducing! Yes, that's right, folks, our very own little human curveball is beating that too! Early days, but every day she gets stronger is another day she's beating the adeno. We also, for the first time since the transplant, saw an immune system. Just! 0.02! But it's coming. Towards the end of the week, when the tests are completed, we'll be able to share what this means and what lies ahead. But, honestly, we're in a much better place than we were on Friday. And, as we suspected, we simply had to wait for Sorrelle to do it her way!

Hopefully in a day or two we'll be able to tell you more. For now, she's doing better every day, and after the concerns of Friday, it seems we really have turned a corner.

Have a great evening, all.

Grandpa

20th April 2016

Caption: Just a little something to tell you.

A very good afternoon, everyone. Let's rephrase that. A magical afternoon, everyone. Let me explain.

Since 22nd August 2015, we have been on quite a journey together. I have written; and you have read about good days, bad days and everything in between. I am sure we have laughed together and cried together. I have always tried not to shock you but at the same time to be honest. There have been times I've had to ask for your patience in order to be accurate and to respect Gemma and Dean's wishes.

There have been too many occasions when this horrible disease has come closer to winning than we'd care for, and when all we had was hope. Well, that, and a remarkable team of medics. (I will come to these heroes shortly.)

Gem and Dean have endured a period of their lives any parent would dread. And they've endured it with a spirit, love and understanding that should make us all proud to know and be related to them. As for our hero, she dazzles us on a daily basis. And to consider she's known as much of her young life in hospital as she has out is unfair and unimaginable.

The families who have rallied, supported and loved beyond words are heroes to Gemma and Dean and have been such an important part in getting us to this point. The army of friends from workplaces and old schools, friends of friends … the list is endless. The messages of support, the time spent calling in to see them, the gifts, the collections, the donations. The remarkable Rob Wynn, with his knowledge, compassion and determination, is of another world. We owe him everything. His team of doctors and that supporting cast of amazing men and women driven to save our little hero. The nurses – those daily angels – visiting day and night with a smile, a reassuring arm, a shoulder when we need it and the hourly care of a little girl and their parents. The lady who has no name but who gave Sorrelle the gift of life. She lay in hospital in London and, in effect, donated life. The other mums and dads on the ward who are able to truly understand and support, even when we couldn't find the words. The lost souls who touched us all and whom we will never forget.

Through the dark days, I often wondered what we could really do to beat this and give not just Sorrelle her life back but Gem and Dean theirs too. The answer is right here in this post – you all did it, every one of you. And at the centre of it all, the one person who did the most – a small boat in a big ocean – Sorrelle. A magical little girl, who beat cancer at 18 months. She showed us what bravery is, what determination is, what fighting is. She has taught us the most important thing – that life is fragile, that you can endure and that we must treasure every moment.

Look at the picture and you will understand what today means. Tissues ready, everyone… Sorrelle is officially cancer-free! She has beaten leukaemia! Her transplant has been a success!

I am sure that in a few short weeks she will leave the hospital as an inpatient for the last time. Now we celebrate life, the future and family.

Please, everyone, go hold someone you love. Do it now, don't wait. Enjoy with every fibre of your being the feeling that we are so fortunate to experience. Families love – that's what we do.

There will be more posts as Sorrelle's recovery continues, but today, at almost eight months, we've WON!

Have a wonderful evening, everyone.

Grandpa

22nd April 2016

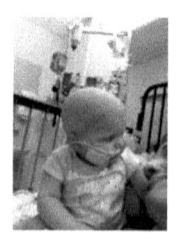

Caption: So, you like these Friday night sleepovers, Grandpa? 😊

A very good evening, everyone. So, the latest Sorrelle news. Well, recovery is ongoing – sluggish would be the best way to describe it. Obviously, it's very easy to get carried away and expect to be home within days, but the watchword here is patience. It will take a few weeks for the transplant to generate the numbers needed to get home. Although the adenovirus dropped a few days ago, the latest tests indicate no change, so on with the medication. As for her white cells and immune system, they've both risen a little and these are now the two important counts. These counts are what indicates recovery and its rate. To give you an idea, a count of 2 on her white cells and .50 on her immune system gets her off the ward. She doesn't go home at that point, but it certainly relaxes isolation and means she can walk around the ward. Currently, her white cells are at 0.5 and her immune system at 0.21. They started at zero, and we're about four days into having signs, so hopefully this gives you an idea of where we're at. She's great in herself, even putting food to her mouth tonight, pinching Grandpa's grapes, then spitting them out. It's a start. She has to learn to trust her throat again after the sores. All moving slowly in the right direction.

Well, my Friday night partner has fallen asleep, so time for my coffee and to gaze at that beautiful sleeping face. For all you parents out there and those still to experience it, you will find nothing better in life than watching a child sleep. It's one of life's wonders.

Have a great evening.

Grandpa

24th April 2016

Caption: How about a Sunday morning smile? 😊

A very good morning, everyone. The first thing I'd like to do is have a bit of a gloat 😊 So, Gemma asks me yesterday, hey, Dad, would you stay with Sorrelle a second night?! It was like winning the lottery 😊 Two nights with the little lady – simply a delight. OK, gloat over, time for the update.

Well, red blood has remained the same – good sign of stability, platelets required, but when you get temperatures, these burn up a lot, so no surprise here. White cells are now .4 – after a slight reduction yesterday, they came back up a little today and that's the same with her immune system, which is currently at .21. The doc is very happy with her progress, albeit slow. As I said before, it's a waiting game, with little steps in the right direction. As for Sorrelle, she's especially smiley this morning and multi-tasked like you wouldn't believe … Snow White, Toy Story, Christmas songs, Peppa Pig and bedtime elephant all on at the same time! It's a good job I love her! The mucositis is finally starting to go, so hopefully we can increase feeds soon and tempt her into eating properly. The picture you see was at 9:30am this morning. What a way to start a day. Right now she's taking a little nap 😊

Enjoy your day, everyone.

Grandpa

25th April 2016

Caption: Psst, Grandpa. What do you reckon – find me some boots and I'm out of here 😊 Wow, Mummy's feet are really this big 😊

A very good evening, everyone, and welcome to tonight's update and smiles. As you can see, our little hero is doin' good. Her smile is getting bigger by the day and the sparkle in her eye is lovely to see. As for her numbers, there's been a slight increase in her white cells to 0.4 and an increase in her immune system to 0.38. You all remember, of course, these are the two important counts now. We await the latest test results on that pesky adenovirus, but it would certainly seem from Sorrelle's numbers and demeanour that it's being held at bay. The latest in terms of getting additional donor cells to boost her immune system is still going ahead. This is simply a precaution and a way of helping her along the recovery path. Gem and Dean had some valuable time with Sorrelle off her lines tonight. You can see such an immediate positive effect on her when this happens. The hope is there will be more of this on a daily basis. The milk feed through tube began again today and so far her stomach has tolerated it, which is another great step. She even managed a bite or two of some crisps. Yet more evidence that the mucositis is at an end, and she is trusting her mouth and throat again.

So, all in all, another good day. We march on, secure in the knowledge that week by week, almost day by day, her condition's improving a little. Still small steps but, hey, it'll be worth the wait 😊

Have a great evening.

Grandpa

27ᵗʰ April 2016

Caption: OK, I look cool, Grandpa – you telling me the truth? 😊

Good evening, all. So, today's news… Well, yo-yo kind of explains it. Temperature up and down, immune system and white cells up and down, and a bit of an unsettled night really. But please remember this isn't surprising the medics at all and they've seen many kids in the same situation. So, if they're not worried, then we're not. Yeah, right! Mums, dads and families worry – it's what we do! Hahaha.

Seriously, though, when she's not spiking temps, she's really happy and up to her usual mischief or just looking adorable. Take last night's picture for example. Even with that contraption on her head, she looks great 😂

Not much more to update really. We get another test result on the adeno tomorrow and hopefully the counts will have an up day. For now, the recovery continues, slowly.

Have a good evening, everyone.

Grandpa

28th April 2016

Caption: A little extra.

Pictures from today, folks. Here's the question. Do you know anyone who could look cuter with a cardboard potty as a hat?!

Our little fashion icon strikes again 😊

Enjoy.

Grandpa

29th April 2016

Caption: A video treat for us all 😊

(Chick-Chick-Chicken Dance)

A very good evening, everyone. So, first, news on Sorrelle's white cells and immune system. Today saw an increase in both! White cells now 1.4 and immune system 1.2 😊 At the same time, the adenovirus has again reduced. Sorrelle's recovery will gather momentum as the increase in her counts impacts on the adenovirus. The medics are now trying to get her off her lines for a little time each day. If the counts don't drop, then there's a chance that after the weekend they will relax her isolation. Sadly, it doesn't mean we open the flood gates, but we can carefully allow visitors. We will have to remain very careful with bugs etc. Please bear with us and hopefully in the next week or two we'll be able to give you good news about this.

The little munchkin had a better night's sleep last night although she's spiking the odd temp – almost for the fun of it! They do the cultures and find nothing. It's almost as though Sorrelle has decided to keep them on their toes. All moving in the right direction and, generally, every day is better than the last. Oh, she does have her mother's stubbornness by the way! 😊

Have a good evening, everyone.

Grandpa

30th April 2016

Caption: Who's giving who the eyes here? 😊

Good evening, everyone. So how have the last couple of days been for our little munchkin? Well, a little up and down to be honest. Her white cells and immune system are still over 1.0, which is very good. The adenovirus is still being treated and remains low enough for the medics to be happy about her progress. There have, however, been temperature spikes and with that comes a higher heart rate. When this happens, they take cultures and see what kind of bug Sorrelle may have picked up – they've all been negative and so the temps are down to the adenovirus. She had a night of broken sleep, so you'd think she'd be feeling pretty down. Well, the picture here was taken today and although she's warm and a bit low, she's still smiling and doing OK. We simply have to persevere and wait for the counts to rise.

There was one lovely development today, though. For the first time, she was allowed out of the room and had a little walk. Small steps but all in the right direction 😊

Have a good evening, everyone.

Grandpa

MAY 2016

3rd May 2016

Caption: So, Mummy, who looks happier to be with who? 😊

Evening, everyone, and welcome to the latest update on our little hero. I know I've used this before but, yet again, it's been up and down and pretty frustrating. The reason, of course, is that now the cancer has gone, we imagined getting home would be a breeze. Truth is, that transplant of any form is a significant treatment and takes time to recover from. High temperatures, high heart rate, infection and, on top of this, the symptoms from the chemotherapy all mean that patience is needed – and lots of it. Finally, of course, you throw in what we call the "Sorrelle surprise" and you begin to realise why we will be here for a number of weeks yet.

Sorrelle's trying to stay happy and isn't too bad. Her counts are steady and rising, albeit slowly. Most importantly, the adenovirus has reduced by a fair chunk and so things remain on the right path. Of course, there are natural frustrations when she feels low, and we then question whether everything is being done. I guess when you reflect, you realise that the medics are still working wonders and we just have to ride out the storms. I remember at the very start of this journey suggesting we would be the ones with the issues and that Sorrelle would just get on with it! Turns out that's true. The little munchkin is doin' OK, still smiling and she's keeping us all going 😊

She's also decided, with much prompting from Mummy, that Grandpa "chatters" a lot! Think we'll be having words when Grandpa sleeps over on Friday 😊

Keep the messages coming for Gem and Dean, please. That room is a pretty lonely place, especially during isolation.

Take care, everyone.

Grandpa

7th May 2016

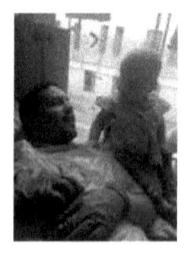

Caption: So, Dad, this Europe thing … you in or out? 😊

Good morning, all. Here we are for the latest update on our little hero. First, her numbers. Well, we have 1.3 white cells and 1.01 immune, so they've both risen from yesterday. Her blood and platelets are being topped up as needed and aren't as important as the immune and the adenovirus readings. The adenovirus, as we all know, is a pretty strong one and not unusual in transplant patients. The better news is that the very high heart rate and temp Sorrelle has had for over a week have suddenly stopped for the last 24 hours. This has meant she's slept properly for the last two nights. And last night with yours truly at the helm was a piece of cake! She slept from 5pm to 8:30am this morning, with a half-hour break for a chat with Mummy on FaceTime! And she's started to drink! And I don't mean sips – proper gulps. She's trusting her mouth and throat again. This is really good stuff. We're winning the little battles which will ensure, God willing, we win the war.

It's very easy to assume that adeno causes fever and if there's no fever, there's no adeno. If only it were that simple. But I'm not one for coincidence, so we're certainly heading in the right direction. What we do now is turn a good 36 hours into 72, and then 72 into 144. You get the drift 😊

Gem and Dean are having a much-needed rest, so it's Grandma at the helm tonight. It's taking longer and it's a bumpy road, but our little hero is getting there. We're waiting for the latest adeno results, which, Rob tells us, are on a downward trend. As soon as we have them, I will let you know.

Sorrelle had much more sparkle in her eyes today. I think she still needs to catch up on sleep, but she's as funny as ever and the staff can't get enough of her. Her heart rate's normal, her temp's normal, her attitude's her mother's! Oops, that slipped out 😊 In short, she's doin' good.

For now, keep everything crossed (well, only the things that don't cause you discomfort haha), keep the messages coming and I'll update you again in a few days. I'll be changing shifts with Grandma soon and warning her she could well be in for a pretty quiet night 😊

Take care, all.

Grandpa

11th May 2016

Caption: Hey, Mummy. I'm thinking this is what real love looks like 😊

Hello, everyone. Time for the latest Sorrelle update. Well, we're still in hospital and there's every likelihood we'll be here for some time yet.

Let me reassure you that Sorrelle's organs are all fine and functioning normally. The adenovirus is reducing, and her immune system is there, albeit low. Getting the balance right here is the trick – treating the virus while letting her immune system grow at a rate her body can tolerate. Imagine, if you will, her immune system having a good look around her body and making sure it likes everything and can live with them. If this were to happen too fast, the new immune system could make a mistake and pick on something that's perfectly harmless. They're getting that balance right and tinkering with it all the time. I hope this helps you understand why this is a long process. Given the medics have seen this all before, it's more normal for them than it is for us. We also need to remember that this is separate from the cancer – that part of the journey is over (apart from the checks). Oh, by the way, great news on that front … this month's STR test again shows no cancer!

And so we continue on the road of transplant, treatment of the virus, and plotting the correct rate of growth for Sorrelle. She's off colour with tummy cramps and given she's been a bit of a chemistry set for the last nine months, it's no surprise she gets unwell. The good news is her smile is still there and she's drinking. Her temperature hasn't spiked as often in the past week, and her heart rate's been normal.

Rob and his medical team are taking great care of the little munchkin. It's all about time, patience, determination, strength and, of course, the greatest ingredient – love. I know I'm biased, but if there are any organisations out there looking for a picture that fully captures the love of a mother and daughter in challenging times, they couldn't do better than this one!

We'll have more news on the adenovirus levels tomorrow, and I'll let you know how that's progressing. For now, enjoy the picture and please keep the messages coming to Gem and Dean. Have a good evening, everyone.

And just to give you all a smile at my expense… Sorrelle's latest trick, when she hears my voice, is to push her thumb and forefinger together in a crab pincer movement while Mummy says "Chatter, chatter, chatter"! Yes, that's right, my 18-month-old granddaughter is telling me to shut up because I talk too much! 😆

We will be chatting, that's for sure! 😆

Grandpa

14th May 2016

Caption: Pretty cosy in here 😊

Good evening, everyone. Time for the latest news on our little hero. Well, last night was a Grandpa sleepover, so I was once again lucky enough to spend time with the little munchkin. First, let's update you on the numbers – just those that matter. The adenovirus reading has fallen to 5.5 from the initial 7.8 five weeks ago. To put this into context, things will be better when this reading is down to 3, at which point treatment won't be necessary. Sounds like another five-week wait but given the rate at which it's dropped in the last two weeks, we could be at the magic 3 in three weeks. Her immune system's hovering between 0.5 and 1.2, and she's OK in herself – a little tired and she's had a bug in her tummy, which is now getting better. Having a transplant is a whole new challenge and has its own roller coasters – without a regular dose of the "Sorrelle Factor"! She's in good hands, though. Given the slow nature of her immune system growth and the adenovirus getting in the way, Sorrelle will be given some more donor cells at the end of May. We have a provisional date of the 25th. Hopefully this boost should see it start to really kick in.

The picture tonight is from yesterday. You can see she's doing OK, but we still have a way to go. Her heart rate is good, and her temperature is settling down. Gem and Dean continue to be a tower of strength – and all this with the arrival of Olivia pretty soon! What remarkable people they are.

Thank you all for your messages. They really do mean so much. It's proving to be a very long process and by its nature a pretty lonely one, so the messages are a real chance for them to take time out and lean on your wonderful support.

We are due another adeno result on Tuesday and so I'll give you the next update then.

Enjoy your evening.

Grandpa

18th May 2016

Caption: Time to bang that drum, Mummy – things are looking up 😊

A very good evening, all. We were due a result on the adenovirus yesterday, but due to problems in the lab, it was delayed to today… We've been waiting patiently all day for it and guess what – it's not arrived! A little frustrating, but that frustration's been tempered by an improvement in Sorrelle's condition and so when the result does arrive (tomorrow), we'll be quite surprised if it hasn't reduced.

Today's numbers represent the best so far overall. The lymphocytes are at their highest and must be having some effect on the virus. I can honestly say that I haven't seen Sorrelle this happy since before her transplant. She's got a real sparkle back. She's drinking, eating a little, no temperature in nearly three days, heart rate perfect, breaths per minute back to normal, oxygen levels good, and they're even starting to remove some of the antibiotics. All in all, some excellent progress being made, in preparation for the additional cells next Wednesday.

There have been some mountains to climb these past few weeks. Happily, our little hero bounces back time and time again. She's the bravest and strongest little girl I have ever come across. As I suspected, she's the one who would show us the way through this treatment. The doctors and nurses are very happy with her condition and although we still await the adeno result, I am sure we're heading in the right direction and will beat it soon enough. I'll update you all as soon as we have the result.

Once again, thank you so much for your messages of support and expressions of love for Gem, Dean and Sorrelle. It honestly does make their time on the ward a little easier. We had the music team in yesterday, which Munchie enjoyed. She continues to drive us all crazy with nursery rhymes! All in all, a very good few days 😊

Take care, all.

Grandpa

21st May 2016

Caption: A cosy night in with Grandpa 😊

Well, a very good evening to you all out there and welcome to the latest update. Let's hit you with a few numbers first. 274 – the number of days since diagnosis! 39 – the number of weeks our little hero has been fighting. 2 – the number of amazing parents she has. 4.8 – adeno DOWN! 132 – heart rate normal! 30 – breaths per minute normal! 52 – days since transplant. And countless – the number of hearts she's warmed!

So, all in all, what can we conclude? It's been a long journey, and we still have a little way to go. We've turned a corner, and Sorrelle has once again confounded the medics and marches on. It really is true, folks. They don't know what on earth she's playing at! You can be assured the data they have from our little hero's reactions and recoveries would fill a medical journal alone!

As you can see from the pictures, Grandpa has the night shift, after Grandma doing the Friday slot and, by all accounts, having fun and lots of sleep 😃 There's been fun tonight too. As I write this, Sorrelle is fast asleep, and I suspect there won't be a peep until tomorrow morning. Things really are looking better, and on Wednesday she'll receive some additional donor cells, which should see her improve even further and get her nearer to coming home. The adeno result is really positive – from a scary high of 7.8, we can see light at the end of the tunnel.

Oh, I forgot a number for you: 1 – very lucky Grandpa 😃

Will update again in a few days. Have a great evening, everyone, and I know I keep saying it, but thank you for your messages of love and support. They mean so much.

Grandpa x

25th May 2016

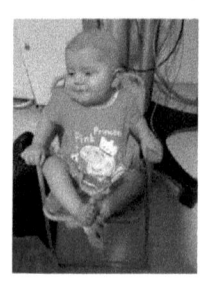

Caption: Easy peasy, this medication lark 😃

Good evening, everyone, and welcome to the latest Sorrelle news. First, let me apologise for the delay. We've been waiting for the adeno result, and knowing that the extra cells were planned for today, I thought it a good idea to do one big update.

Sorrelle is in great shape. It's true we've had some scary moments in the last few weeks, but it seems that's behind us. A couple of weeks ago, this dreaded adenovirus was at 6.8 and was causing swelling to her bowel, which, in turn, was pressing on her lungs, making her breathe quickly. The measurement of the swelling was 5.9, and all her numbers were low. She was pretty poorly for a spell. Compare that, however, with today, when the adeno figure is 4.4, swelling 2.7 and all other numbers rising. New cells have been infused, and she's eating and drinking. And more than anything else, she's happy! The sparkle gets brighter every day, and when I was with her Monday night, she was simply a joy. It's the only reason I was able to get on a plane yesterday for a holiday. The doctors are really happy with her and even talking about getting her home in the next few weeks! Now we all know medicine and we all know the Sorrelle Factor, but I still reckon we're finally on that last stretch home. I won't lie, it's been the most difficult period by far, but this little girl has the ability to bounce back, prove them all wrong, amaze, delight, and make us smile.

A really great day. A final thought to leave you with… When you message Gem and Dean, please make mention of a very special lady. She'll probably never see these posts, and we'll probably never know her name, but in short she saved a little girl, she saved a family, she gave hope where there was despair, and she allowed us to restore our belief in the spirit of goodness. If you ever see this – from a very humble and emotional grandpa, thank you for making my family whole.

Have a great evening, everyone. I'm speaking to Gem daily and will update you on the progress, especially now after the new cells.

I have one more treat for you – a video from Monday with Sorrelle doing what Sorrelle does best. That'll be cuteness 😊

Take care, all.

Grandpa

27th May 2016

Caption: Go on then, Mummy, give us a kiss 😊

Good evening, all, and once again to the fully paid-up members of the Sorrelle fan club, welcome to the latest update. So, as we head into the weekend, nearly eight weeks since transplant, we find ourselves still battling away and continuing to beat whatever hiccups come along. Today's numbers are a little lower overall but stable. The latest pesky adeno result is a fraction higher, at 4.7, but we have seen this kind of fluctuation before, and there's no great concern as the general trend is downward. The additional cells have been infused, and we wait for these to graft to the previous transplant.

So, what does this all mean for the days and weeks ahead? Well, some pretty good news. Rob (Sorrelle's professor) had a chat with Gem and Dean today and set out what he would like to see happen over the next couple of weeks – obviously, the graft continuing to take, the adenovirus staying under control and Sorrelle tolerating feeds, either orally or via feeding tube. He's upbeat about all three of these measures and, if we continue on the current path, he could have her home in a couple of weeks! Yep, that's right, we're getting real close! 😊 So, all we need is for our little hero to put the curve balls away and for the medicine to stay predictable. We can steer this little boat steady as she goes. We're in a good place right now, and Sorrelle continues to get stronger and her sparkle ever more present. The pictures tell the story.

As always, thank you for the constant stream of lovely messages. Grandma's in the saddle tonight, while Mum and Dad have a little them time. Well, with the bump too 😊

Will keep you updated over the weekend. For now, enjoy your weekends, everyone.

Take care.

Grandpa

JUNE 2016

1st June 2016

Caption: Hey, what's that daft-looking thing on the end of the whistle? Sorrelle asked the bird. Hahaha!

Good afternoon, all, and again apologies for the delay. We were waiting for the adenovirus result, which arrived later due to the bank holiday. We now have it, and it's once again 4.4, which, given that medication across the board is being reduced now, is very good. The medical team are very happy. Sorrelle's other numbers have risen a little today also, so her immune measure is now .79 and her white cells 1.3. Her blood and platelets are good although she's needing platelet top-ups every couple of days. This won't be required once the counts rise, and they say that the second set of cells donated should start to show through in around another week.

As with her time on the cancer ward, it takes a little time for her stomach to tolerate food in increasing quantities and so there's a period of up and down between oral nutrition and the nose tube feeds. The oral feeding is continuing as this is less intrusive for our little hero and she's obviously happier with it. As for her general demeanour, she is happy, cheeky, playing, missing Grandpa obviously haha, and the sparkle is evident. If this rate of improvement continues, the plan is for her to leave hospital as an inpatient and return to the day clinic as needed, which will be pretty often at the beginning. But to sleep in her own bed and know that her home life can begin once again is a wonderful thing.

We get the next adeno result late on Friday and so that'll be the next update, folks. It only remains for me to thank you once again for your support and to ask you to continue sending in those messages.

And to Dean – my humble apologies for the caption. You really can't give me bullets like that and expect me not to fire them! 😂

Take care, all.

Grandpa

3rd June 2016

Caption: Yes, Lord Vader, you're right – the cute force is strong in this one 😊

A very good evening, everyone. Once again, here we are gathered for the latest news on the little munchkin. As you can see from the picture, she's up and about, there's a smile on that little face and she's off her wires 😊 The wires are now on for less time, while the medication continues to reduce and she feeds more. Means she can at least start to build her muscles and use those little legs.

So, as for the latest set of numbers and what they mean… That dreaded adenovirus has remained at 4.4, which means her body is doing more of the work to suppress it. She'll continue to receive special medication for the virus alone and so, as her other numbers continue to increase, the adeno will reduce. Her other numbers are good. White cells up, immune system up and blood and platelets, whilst dropping, are doing so more slowly, which again shows her second set of cell donation has the rumblings of working. The doctors have now started her on penicillin, to protect and enhance her own immune system. The really great news is this is the first step the doctors take before sending you home!

And so to the really good stuff. Again, taking into account the Sorrelle Factor, even that shouldn't stop us from getting her home VERY soon! My guess – before her little sister arrives 😊 There's ongoing work with her food intake to ensure she gets the right level of food. This will all be sorted ready for home time. As I've mentioned before, it's very likely that Sorrelle will visit as a day case for some time, but at least she'll be returning to some form of normal home life, the one we all take for granted. The next adeno result should be on Wednesday, so I'll update you fully then, with a little catch-up beforehand.

The only emotion right now is happiness – finally, our little hero is nearer to the life we all want for her. Her mum and dad get to share the simple magic of watching their child sleep in their own bed, toddle around the house, throw food out of the high chair, cause chaos with crayons, bounce on their bed when they want to sleep. Kinda crazy that these are now things we look forward to Sorrelle, Gem and Dean experiencing. Most of all, I'm looking forward to the hospital staff missing her, if you know what I mean. They've been treated to this special little girl for long enough. Now it's our turn!

Take care, everyone.

Grandpa

9th June 2016

Caption: Oh my you mean I haven't told you? 😊

A very good evening, everyone. I must apologise for the delay in your Sorrelle update. I arrived back in the UK last night and I didn't get the adeno result until 2am, at which point I had a choice of post or sleep. Sleep won!

So, here we are, 70 days on from the start of the bone marrow journey and at long last, we're starting to see some very significant improvements across the board. Her white cells are the highest they've been, at over 2.0, the immune measure rose above 2.0 for the first time, and the adeno result has shown yet another reduction, at now 4.0. Her red blood's actually increased and her platelets remain steady. Sounds amazing, hey 😊 And just at that point, our little tease throws one of her curve balls at us, spikes a temp for the first time in three weeks, burns platelets like they're going out of fashion and is sick! Well, Munchie, thanks for keeping us all on our toes. Now if you'd like to get back to being medically boring, we would appreciate it! Hahaha.

Counts still good today and when I visited her this evening, all she did was laugh and eat! Honestly, everyone, it's the best I've seen her since before going onto the bone marrow ward. And as I reported last time, she's very quickly moving to getting home. Rob said today he's really happy with her and now needs to get her home. Could be next week if everything continues moving in the direction it is. Gem and Dean are looking a little happier and can start looking forward to having Sorrelle home soon, before Olivia's arrival. It's all close enough to touch, and her improvement has begun a momentum that won't stop now – or it certainly seems that way. They will spend the next few days assessing her food intake and put in place any assistance with this, along with her daily visits to the clinic for treatment.

Oh, one final delightful little event to share with you all. I received a 20-second video with the first official muttering of "Grandpa"! Safe to say Kleenex are now offering me shares in the company! What a delight it is the moment you know you are more than a noise and you have that special name 😊

So, the next adeno result should be Friday, and I have a hospital stay booked in with the little munchkin, so I will update you all then. Who knows, we may even have a date when Sorrelle can begin to experience the cosy warmth of home.

Take care, everyone.

Grandpa

12th June 2016

Caption: Getting better means play time!

Good afternoon, everyone. I have some pretty good news, some so-so news and some very good news. So, first, the pretty good news. The adeno has increased just a little but is still only 4.3, which is really good when we consider that Sorrelle was under the weather earlier in the week and again yesterday and today. That brings me to the so-so news, which is to say that her tummy is a little sore and getting it to work properly after so long is proving frustrating. To be honest, before her diagnosis, Sorrelle had a bit of a tricky bowel, which alas runs in the family. So, it was always likely that with this treatment she would have periods where she gets sore or a little swollen. Importantly, she's not in any danger …

and this is where the very good news is. Our little hero's not only happy but her numbers are, frankly, amazingly normal!

Let me take you through them. White cells are 8.6 and the normal range is between 6 and 17. Her red blood count is 139 and the normal range is 101 to 138. And her immune is now 6.97! The normal range is between 1 and 5, which basically means that not only is there no leukaemia but that the bone marrow transplant has worked! So, apart from the sore tummy and establishing her eating pattern, she's wonderfully well. They will monitor her stomach and put necessary treatment in place. My guess is that getting her home may take a couple more weeks but, hey, Sorrelle constantly baffles us, so it would be tomorrow if she had her way! Hahaha. And so the cycle continues. We have another adeno result on Tuesday, when I reckon we'll have a better idea of how her tummy is doing and some kind of time frame to getting her home. Friday night with her was simply a delight and she is getting happier by the day. Yes, she's uncomfortable with her tummy, but compared to what she's already beaten, this is a walk in the park 😊

I will post another update on Tuesday, when we have the next adeno result.

Take care, everyone.

Grandpa

13th June 2016

Caption: Newsflash! Read all about it, folks 😊

A very good evening, everyone. A little extra update for you this evening, with some pretty lovely news. First, Sorrelle's numbers are very good and she's been in great spirits today. She had some time off her lines and we went to explore. And this is where the really good news comes … Sorrelle is now officially out of isolation! 😊 It's taken a long time, and we've certainly had some ups and downs, but given her numbers, the hospital see no reason to keep her in strict isolation any longer.

And so what does this mean for all of you reading this? It simply means you can now visit Sorrelle! You will remember me mentioning she seems to have the Price bowel thing, and so they're going to take a biopsy tomorrow and try and sort that out for her. Tube feeding has been put back to the end of next week most probably and once she's tolerating that, it'll be home time 😊

So, as for the visiting, everyone is, of course, welcome, but please contact Gemma and Dean directly. It's very important you don't just turn up. First, it would be too much for Sorrelle and second, it's a small and very strict ward for obvious reasons. Gem, Dean and Sorrelle will be delighted to see you, and after three months of isolation it will be a wonderful new experience, but they do need to be able to arrange your visits.

I will update tomorrow with the latest adeno results and let you know how the little munchkin is. So, enjoy tonight's lovely news and have a good evening.

Grandpa

14th June 2016

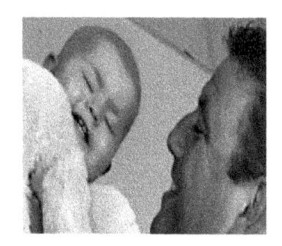

Caption: Yep, Grandpa, I'm pretty happy 😊

Good evening, everyone. As promised, an update on our little hero. Sorrelle's biopsy went just fine. She came round sleepy but happy and is totally OK. We will have the results in the next day or so and we don't expect there to be any major issues. If there are any problems with her bowel, we can get it treated.

So, again, today, she's had a little food and been very happy – as you can see in tonight's picture. The adeno result is now down to 4.1, so everything's moving in the right direction and we're another day nearer to getting her home. The sickness she's had over the last week has delayed going home, but it's getting closer. Oh, and just to throw you another Sorrelle curve ball, last night she achieved a personal best temperature – a small matter of 40.5. And then, get this – totally fine this morning! She really is a character! Pretty lovable too 😊 She's getting better day by day and is a very happy little girl. Almost a year on, we haven't just survived, we've grown stronger, humbler, more resilient and more understanding. When you think you're going to crumble, you find the strength from somewhere to go on. And if you get your wish, the day arrives when you can begin to plan and imagine all of those things to come. Home is the next step and then, well, that's the next chapter 😊

Please let Gem or Dean know if you would like to visit and they will arrange a time for you.

Next adeno result is Friday, and so I will update you all again then.

Have a good evening, everyone.

Grandpa

17th June 2016

Caption: Round like a circle in a spiral 😊

A very good evening, everyone. Quite a bit of info for you tonight. So, Tuesday and Wednesday were pretty good days. Our little hero was on top form, giggling and being her usual adorable self, her counts remained pretty constant and high, and all was well with the world … so well that there was talk of letting her go home Saturday night or Sunday, just for the day. So, true to form, the sickness returned as soon as there was a sniff of home! Haha, yep, the Sorrelle Way was at it again. She's still been pretty perky, though there appears to be an infection in her line. And so yesterday, after a lovely little spell at the park across the road from the hospital, Gem returned to be told no weekend leave and that Sorrelle would need the infected line removing today and a new one putting in on Monday. What this means is that the antibiotics can now get rid of the bug without the line retaining it. It's frustrating and it's put back her being discharged, but our little hero has to be bug-free when they let her leave. Theatre today was fine and we are sure that Sunday will be fine too.

As for her numbers today, they're a tiny bit lower but still high compared to last week. And it seems that the days of low numbers are gone, which is great. We have the latest adeno result, which is standing at 4.2 – a very slight increase but not surprising given the infection. I'm sure that once the infection has gone, it'll reduce. It's important to remember she's in really good spirits. Gem and Dean are having a night at home and getting a bedroom ready for a new arrival and a return! Exciting times. I left

Gem and Dean's tonight with a warm smile, thinking of them all in the weeks ahead as a family enjoying time at home, happy and healthy – something we must never take for granted.

I'm going to finish tonight's update with a special word for our hero's daddy. As a father, I know only too well the gift of a daughter, and indeed a son, but for the purpose of this, let me focus on daughters. Fathers immediately want to protect their little girls. Most of the time, you can do this, but sadly not all the time – and you feel helpless, useless and frustrated. You beat yourself up thinking, I'm supposed to make it better! What you don't realise is, by simply being a dad you *do* make it better. Being there makes it better, loving them makes it better, supporting them makes it better, holding them makes it better, giggling with them makes it better.

Dean, I know the hell you've been through, and as we approach Father's Day, I want you to know how proud I am of you, as others are too. Despite this roller coaster you've had to endure, you have been there for my daughter and your daughter. So, from one father to another, thank you. And believe me, you did the dad thing – you *did* make it better. You only have to look at Sorrelle smiling at you to know.

Well, everyone, have a great weekend. I will update again on Tuesday, which is the next adeno result day.

Grandpa

22nd June 2016

Caption: If you go down to the woods today, you're sure of a big surprise – the bears are all in hospital!

A very good evening, everyone, and here we are again with our Sorrelle update. So, the adenovirus has fallen slightly to 4.1. This is very good considering Sorrelle has still got a little sickness. I think the reason it's still low is down to her immune count, which is nice and high, and because her white cells are very good. Her new line was put in on Monday, together with a gastric tube, which allows for feeding. She's taking a few days to get over that but, as you can see from yesterday's picture, she's still well and enjoying a new addition to her soft toy collection. My wonderful workmates at our St Helen's office very kindly bought this bear for her. Your kindness and messages of support for Gem, Dean and Sorrelle really make a huge difference. Cancer wards and bone marrow wards can be very lonely places, so to have the support of so many people is wonderful. Thank you, one and all.

The plan for Sorrelle is to tolerate feeds through the new tube, and then the next stage is home – hopefully just before Olivia is born! She is due on 16th July, so it's gonna be mighty close, that's for sure! We are closer than ever to a home life and a new kind of normal 😊

I will update again on Friday when we receive the next adeno result.

Take care, all.

Grandpa

25th June 2016

Caption: Sorry, Peppa, bacon is bacon, and I haven't eaten properly in months 😊

A very good evening, everyone, and welcome to the latest update on our little hero. First, let's update you on the numbers. Adeno is steady at 4.1 – and the test was taken while Sorrelle was still a little under the weather, so we are sure it'll reduce next week. She hasn't been sick in days or had a temperature, and her sparkly smile is back to full strength. Her red blood has just been topped up for the first time in a week, so the signs are good that there's increasing stability there too. Platelets also just been topped up. Her white cell count is just under 3, as is her immune system, but, importantly, she's now off any booster drugs and so these counts are all of her own making. The gastro tube is settling and not causing any discomfort, and for the first time it really feels that home is very close.

They even let her go home for the day today, and I've just brought her back for the night. She's been full of fun and smiles all day and she got to see her own bedroom for the first time in nearly four months! I don't have the words to describe the intense delight at seeing Gem and Dean with her at home. It convinced me that home is the medicine she needs. Hopefully, this will be a permanent dose in a week or so. That would be my guess based on how well she's doing. The cancer's gone, the transplant was a success, the adenovirus is under control, her temperature's normal, the bugs have all gone, she's happy, and she had a day trip home. I think you'll agree this is the stuff of dreams. That discharge day is almost here, and her childhood will soon be renewed. The bell is ever closer and a new chapter's about to begin.

So, back to my evening with the little superstar, which I suspect will be pretty quiet as she'll sleep until morning now. What she doesn't know is the joy she gives me while I watch her sleep 😊

I will update you with the next adeno result, on Tuesday. Until then, enjoy the weekend.

Grandpa

29th June 2016

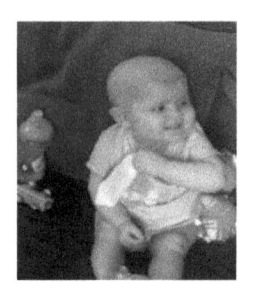

Caption: It's my tissue and I'll smile if I want to.

Good morning, everyone, and welcome to day 313 of the Sorrelle journey. Her numbers are really good today. Her white cell count and immune system continue to grow, and her red blood and platelets are becoming more stable every day. The adeno has risen slightly to 4.2, but this is under control and poses no threat to her. The doctors are very happy with her, and she has just started to tolerate the gastro tube feeding, albeit in small amounts. She's now allowed out of the hospital for the day as long as she doesn't spike a temperature, so guess what she did last night … yep, you guessed it, she spiked a temperature! Ah, those lovely Sorrelle curve balls! At least she was able to be there for Gemma's surprise baby shower last Sunday. It was a joy to see her in a home environment and with her two little cousins too 😊

And so we keep going towards the day when she comes home for good and becomes an outpatient. Hopefully not long to go now.

Will update Friday, with the next adeno. Until then, take care, all.

Grandpa

JULY 2016

2nd July 2016

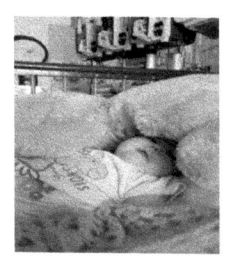

Caption: Cosy with Doggie

Good morning, everyone, and a warm welcome to the latest instalment of the Sorrelle Times. We've received the latest adeno result, which is unchanged at 4.2. Pretty happy with this considering the curve ball she threw earlier in the week with spiking temps, vomiting and her heart rate back up at 200+! Bless her haha. Thankfully, this has all calmed down again, notably after Gemma left for a break. This kid really does pick her moments!

So, this morning, she's been laughing, playing, had lots to drink and all seems to be normal again. The remaining issue is her eating. She's still not tolerating the gastro tube, and so they'll keep tinkering with ratios until we hit the right one. Yesterday she managed to eat a little orally, and, of course, they have her on chemical feeds, which give her body everything she needs. It's now a case of getting her stomach to work, which will take time after it being unused. We're getting nearer to getting her home for good, and although it's frustrating for Gem and Dean, she is in the best place, and they don't get hung up on days or dates. All they care about is Sorrelle being well enough to be let home – and we should thank them for that. Her other numbers are consistently good and stable. It's a waiting game to managing her feeding and getting home 😊

Rob, the other doctors and all the nurses have spent almost a year devoted to the cure and care of our little hero. I have seen them smile with her, care for her, cure her cancer, get her through her transplant, and cry at times too. She has struck a chord with everyone she's come into contact with, and so the most reassuring thing for us is that our little munchkin will be discharged when all these heroes know she is safe. That, with Mummy and Daddy's love, is all she needs. Maybe this team should've taken on Iceland!

Have a great weekend.

Grandpa

6th July 2016

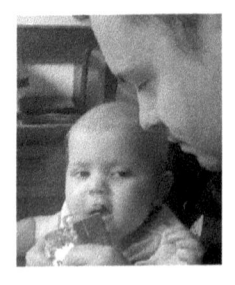

Caption: Out for a drink with my dad 😊

A very good morning, everyone. Let me give you an overview of where we are at and the getting home situation. Sorrelle's stomach and bowel aren't yet working as they should. We have these hairs that absorb food and drink and allow us to digest properly. Sorrelle's have been a bit battered and so when she picks up a bug and we try to feed her or give her liquid feeds, nothing absorbs because there's nothing to stick to inside. It's kinda like going on a slide as a kid. If it's shiny, you whizz straight down and off! Basically, we need Sorrelle's gut to stop being shiny! However, there have been signs in the last couple of days that she's keeping things down, which means the bugs are reducing and consequently she's feeling better, laughing more and her counts are rising! Red counts and platelets are now rising on their own without top-ups, her immune system has risen, and the adeno has reduced to 4.0, which is great news.

It is frustrating and we want her home but that will not happen until the medics are happy her gut is stable. Typically, this can take many months after transplant and at the moment that's the only timescale we have. I think the best way to approach this is to acknowledge that beating cancer and coming through transplant, along with all the bugs and problems, is more than enough to celebrate for now – and she is here with us, safe. There are parents on these wards who won't get to experience the future that we are so fortunate to know is around the corner.

Sorrelle's allowed off the ward and so she can enjoy quality time with Mum and Dad. As I seem to be saying on a regular basis, patience is key.

I will update again at the weekend with the next adeno.

Have a good day, all.

Grandpa

7th July 2016

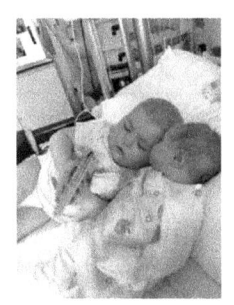

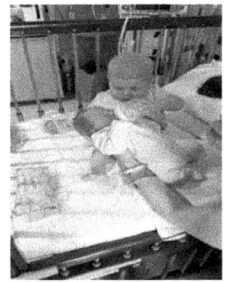

Caption: Sisters are doing it for themselves!

A very good morning, all, and welcome to a very special update. Meet Sorrelle's little sister, Olivia Hope. Olivia joined us last night, weighing in at a very healthy 8lb 1oz. Sorrelle, as you can see, is captivated by her sister, as we all are. It's the medicine we all need. Here's to a lifetime of love, laughter and joy.

Have a great day, everyone.

Grandpa

8th July 2016

Caption: Hey, Grandpa, my sparkle's back 😊

So, a very good evening to you all, after what has been quite a few days. You will all know our little hero now has the tag of 'big sister' to the gorgeous Olivia. It has been wonderful to see them together and even though she's only been here two days, she's already proving to be that missing medicine Sorrelle needed! Sorrelle is so besotted with her, it's almost distracted her from being poorly. She is so excited that she has a positive energy all the time. I honestly thought when I saw her a couple of days ago that this might happen. And she has got much better – she has a wonderful sparkle in her eyes and a smile to match.

So, what has this meant for her numbers? Well, they're all stable and improving … and the best bit … the adeno result is down to its lowest level of 3.7! This really is fantastic news, because the lower the measurement, the easier it is for her body to fight what's left. So, there you have it – the medication and the transplant are essential, but never underestimate the power of a new little sister arriving to keep you positive 😊 The end is finally in sight. Maybe Olivia was the last piece of the puzzle in getting our little hero home.

Tonight, I have the pleasure of the night shift while Gem, Dean and Olivia rest at home. Hopefully, in the near future, the family of four can finally plan, dream and be together. It has been quite a journey. My thoughts now turn to imagining two sisters together, hearing that end of treatment bell ring!

Have a great weekend, everyone. I'll update again with the next adeno result, on Tuesday.

Grandpa

12th July 2016

Caption: Come on, Sis, let's escape 😊

Good evening, everyone, and welcome to the latest update on the progress of our little hero. As you can see from the picture, Olivia has captivated her big sister. If I had to sum things up in one word, it would be inseparable! After so long on this journey, I don't believe in coincidence. There has been a definite improvement since her little sister's arrival. The adenovirus went down to 3.7 from 4.2, which is the biggest fall in six weeks – and that was just after Olivia arrived 😊 And today it has dropped again from 3.7 to 3.3! I can't tell you how amazing this is. Usually, the medics are happy with a .5 reduction in a week. This last week has almost doubled that, and the doctors are delighted. All the other numbers are also higher, as they'd expect for her body to fight the adeno. Her immune reading is over 3, her white cells are high and her red blood count is still rising on its own. So that leaves us with the main issue of her tummy. They've done some tests, and she has reflux, which can now be combatted with medication. Her bowel is still a little swollen, and these things together are responsible for the sickness. With medicine, we feel sure she can start tolerating liquid feeds over the next few days. The good news is that solid foods are starting to interest our little hero, and she seems able to keep them down.

So, to sum up, we're getting real close, folks! She's laughing and is happy, she loves her sister to bits, she's starting to eat, the adeno is reducing, the cancer has gone, the transplant has worked, she's getting nearer to going home and she continues to wow everyone who comes into contact with her. She was even able to spend some time out of hospital on Sunday and give our American family who are visiting a big surprise. A lovely day and so wonderful to see her happy with family. It's what grandpas dream of.

Well, have a great evening, everyone. I will update you again on Friday when we've received the next adeno result.

Take care.

Grandpa

17th July 2016

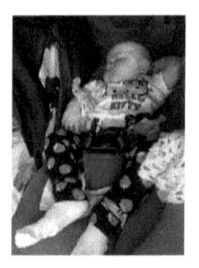

Caption: Tiring work being a superstar 😊

Good afternoon, everyone. I apologise for the late post, but the adeno result was late yet again. The good news, however, is it's now 3.2. Sorrelle has been let out of hospital during the day and returns overnight for her chemical feed. This will continue until they're able to set this up at home and then discharge her to outpatient. We continue to work on her eating but, as yet, she still only has sporadic interest. Over time, as her tummy heals, she will find it easier and more pleasant to eat. Until then, they will ensure she receives all the nutrients her body needs. We are in an altogether different and much better place than in previous months. A little frustrating she's still not home, but we should count our blessings that she is well and showing constant improvement.

This has, as you all know, been a long and upsetting journey. The nature of what Sorrelle and we as a family have fought has meant there have been highs and lows. We've spoken of the brave, beautiful children Sorrelle has grown up with, and their amazing families, who have supported us, as we have them. We have all become a larger family fighting a common enemy.

Heartbreakingly, some of these battles have been lost. You will recall me mentioning a very special little boy called Charlie, who we became very close to. Sadly, last week, Charlie became one of those brave angels looking down on us from on high, now free from pain and at peace. I want to pay tribute to Charlie's amazing mum and family. Charlie's mum was the first parent on Ward 84 I spoke to when Sorrelle was diagnosed. Her patience, understanding and warmth were a real comfort, and she and her family have been a great support to Gemma and Dean. They are remarkable people. I hope you will keep them in your thoughts and prayers at this terrible time. They will always be a part of this family, and we will always remember that brave little boy with his special smile and eyes that would light up a room. Rest peacefully, little man xx

Take care, everyone.

Grandpa

19th July 2016

Caption: Hmm… Pigs live in books and this one's real? Yeah sure, Grandpa!

A very good afternoon, everyone, and here we are once again for the Sorrelle update. There's not much to tell, other than the adeno is down yet again, at 3.1! We're winning, folks, and with each lower result we are nearer to her tummy feeling better and nearer to eating. And we all know what that means – discharge to outpatient. Although the road is long, there has been real progress. I truly believe the days of bad viruses are behind us. I say that with the understanding that Sorrelle wasn't supposed to get leukaemia! But life sadly doesn't come with guarantees. Live for the day, cherish what you have and cherish all the memories it gives you.

Today, Sorrelle returns to where it began, on Ward 84. Not because of any returning cancer but because the transplant bed is needed. There are no isolation rules, and Gem and Dean's time there will be a little freer. There are old familiar faces there, who I suspect will love seeing Sorrelle again 😊 So, once more, on to Friday, hopeful for another adeno reduction. In the meantime, onward and upward, as they say.

Have a good evening, all.

Grandpa

23rd July 2016

Caption: So, there I was in the bag with a bag, when I thought, I got this in the bag!

Caption: Yeah, I'm so cool. Gimme five, cuz 😊

Good evening, everyone. The adeno result is late coming back and probably won't be available until tomorrow morning, but I thought I'd give you an update anyway. I have a feeling when they ring for the test result something must get lost in translation. It does rather sound like a "dunno"! Time for yet more patience! And for those who know me, when it comes to my family, this grandpa ain't blessed with a lot of that! Luckily, one gaze at our little hero and I calm in an instant 😊

So, the last few days. One word – great. Sorrelle is now allowed away from the hospital daily and returns overnight for her chemical feed. Sounds like she's a bunch of flowers, bless her! Anyway, her counts are all good and still consistent, which means her stomach's continuing to recover. She will hopefully tolerate feeds soon and can then be discharged from the ward and move to outpatient status. It's a slow process, but she's getting better daily and that's gotta be good enough. It's worth remembering she has no cancer, the transplant has worked and the donor cells have totally replaced her old cells. We had the latest MRD result, which is done monthly, to check there's no sign of returning cancer and that's remained negative – and has done for the last three months. Considering where we were almost a year ago, that's remarkable.

Today's caption pictures convey a very happy little girl who's getting closer to that normal life we all crave for her. As a special treat, I will post a few more pictures so you too can enjoy Sorrelle's time off the ward.

Tomorrow, I will post a quick update with the adeno result.

Take care, all.

Grandpa

24th July 2016

Caption: So, Grandpa, when is it he turns into my prince exactly?

When you're 40, Munchkin. Haha!

A very good afternoon, everyone. Sorrelle slept wonderfully for Grandpa again last night, and once the nurses had taken her off her lines, then up the motorway we were for a morning at Grandpa's. As you can see from the picture, she is happy and feeling much more like the Sorrelle we know and love. She managed to taste some toast today, so, who knows, maybe the eating isn't too far away.

Time to give you the geeky numbers. Platelets is 36 (this is getting low, so I guess she will need a top-up in a day or so). Red blood count is 107, which is totally fine. White cells is 5.9, which is fab. Immune system is 4.5, which is in the normal range. Lymphocytes is .55 – these are what fight the adenovirus, along with the medication. I can't tell you just how good these numbers are. It's not that long ago we were seeing most of these measure at less than 1. Sorrelle really is beating everything that's been thrown at her, and she's moving so far down the recovery road it's highly unlikely she'll become really poorly again. Of course, there are never any guarantees in life, as 22nd August last year taught us. But the point is, her numbers are now that good that infections and bugs no longer have the same awful effects as before.

I know what you're thinking – he's forgotten the adeno result. That one result that now means the most for her ongoing recovery. Nope, hadn't forgotten, just thought I'd build the tension a bit 😊 Drum roll … how does 2.9 grab ya! Amazing reduction! Our little hero really is almost there.

Have a great day, everyone. Thank you for your ongoing love and support. We see and read your comments, we see you checking in on the little munchkin, and it is so warming for Gem and Dean to know they're in your thoughts.

Take care, all.

Grandpa

27th July 2016

Caption: Sometimes a girl's just gotta do happy 😊

Good evening, all. A short post tonight to give you more time to soak up today's amazing smile 😊 Our little hero is well, though out of the blue she spiked a temp, so, as a precaution, she's spent the day in hospital. The main reason for the shorter post is the delay of the adeno result. We are, however, expecting another one on Friday anyway and so I will give you all a longer update then. For now, do enjoy the picture – one of the best caption pictures, I reckon. Let's have a vote 😊

Take care, all.

Grandpa

29th July 2016

Caption: Hey, Mummy, look at all those people out there reading this. Shall I tell them about the adeno?

Hi, everyone, and welcome to the latest update on our little munchkin. So, first news is that her numbers are good and stable and that her platelets are increasing on their own. She's happy and playful, but there's still a way to go with her tummy. I had a good, long chat with the doctor this morning about this and her not eating. The problems with her tummy and bowel are pretty normal given her treatment, and I'm afraid they will take some months to repair themselves. There is a keyhole surgical option, but they may decide to let them heal on their own. In any event, the sickness will carry on until her tummy recovers properly. So, before I tell you about the adeno, I just want to remind you that whilst the adeno and the treatment have caused her stomach problems, that doesn't mean that when the adeno finally goes, her stomach will be repaired. Doesn't quite work that way, though that's no bad thing 😊

So, the adeno… Really not sure how to tell you this but … it's nearly gone! Yep, you read that correctly. We're still in shock to be honest. It's the most remarkable news and it puts Sorrelle in a safer place medically than ever! When Sorrelle's adeno was at its worst and measured 7.8, it meant there were literally millions of adeno cells that needed eliminating. It currently measures around 500 units! And the reason for the reading of 2.9 earlier in the week is because the cell number's too small to register. So, she still has it, but it's tiny compared to before. Let's put it this way: if the next downward reading came back saying "negative reading", that would mean gone.

Basically, folks, no cancer, transplant a success and adeno pretty much gone! We are so very lucky. Sorrelle has battled, and given us plenty of scares along the way, but she has almost won the battle back to normal childhood.

I want to take a moment to once again thank her amazing doctors and caring nurses and our loving family and friends. Yep, that means you lot 😊 I have shared many times my thoughts, feelings, hopes and concerns with you all. I've been honest with you, despite not wanting to worry you. Collectively, every one of you has helped Gem, Dean, Sorrelle and now Olivia dream of a family future together away from hospitals, isolations, chemicals, monitors, theatres, treatments, injections and loneliness. A final thanks to Sorrelle, for giving us fun, bravery, courage and inspiration to cope with this journey. The end is very nearly in sight and, today, more than any other, I feel truly blessed and lucky.

Today, Gem, Dean and I were honoured to say a final farewell to little Charlie. I could not let this post pass without mentioning this beautiful little boy and the real treat we all had in spending time with him. We will always remember our little friend, now flying high and watching us with his adorable smile.

Take care, everyone.

Grandpa

AUGUST 2016

3rd August 2016

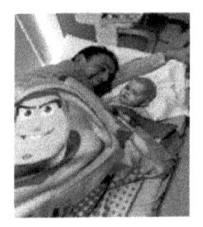

Caption: C'mon, Grandpa, move up a bit 😊

Good morning, everyone, and welcome to the latest Sorrelle update. Well, it would seem our little hero is marching from strength to strength. Her white cells and immune system are in normal range, and her platelets are generating themselves without much need for top-up. It means her body is starting to return to normal, after what has been a long fight. The adenovirus is still at 500, which you will remember is the level at which it is just detectable. It's not posing a threat, so they've now stopped medication for it!

Gemma is being trained on changing lines for the nighttime chemical feeds, and once this is done, then, finally, after almost a year, Sorrelle will be discharged as an outpatient. We are almost there and, in the next couple of weeks, I am sure I'll be able to give you the news we have all been waiting for. Her tummy still has some repairing to do, but the medication for the adeno can aggravate this, which is another reason for stopping it. Already, we're seeing a slight improvement, but do remember it will be some months before Sorrelle is eating normally.

All in all, we carry on, with the sight of the bell shining brightly, almost ready to ring 😊

Will update again with the next adeno result, hopefully Saturday.

Take care, all.

Grandpa

6th August 2016

Caption: Ready to make my escape, but rumbled at the last minute!

Good evening, all, and welcome to the Sorrelle Gazette! Your chance to read up on the progress of our little hero. So, first, her numbers. Well, white cells 8.8, which is brilliant. Immune 4.8 – amazing. Platelets 45 and rising on their own – wonderful. Blood 79 – pretty good, just getting a top-up tonight. And before I update on the adeno result, let me remind you about the lymphocytes, the part of the immune system that fights the adenovirus – this is now reading 1.4, which is great.

So, what does this really mean? You'll remember they stopped medication for the adenovirus, which at that point measured 500 units and was too low to show on the higher count charts. Now, without medication and nothing to fight it, you'd think it would increase, which it would if her immune system and lymphocytes hadn't have carried on the fight. And so, for the first time, Sorrelle's body is keeping the virus at bay on its own. This is a massive achievement. She is now free from ALL medication, and her body is getting stronger. All we're waiting for is for her tummy to repair and for her to eat orally.

In 17 days, it will be exactly one year since diagnosis. The day a little girl faced the fight of her life. A small boat in a big ocean. A family gripped by fear. A year on, we have a little girl with her life in front of her and a family who dare to dream. It is impossible for me to express my joy, relief, gratitude, humbleness and reflection in a single post, but if you've read Sorrelle's story from the start, I hope you'll have a sense of what a monumental year it has been.

And so three things remain – to get her home, get her tummy repaired and ring that bell in celebration. Not just to celebrate Sorrelle but everyone involved in this journey, including you. The condition was diagnosed and treated, but what helped pull it together was you out there. Your love and support has been the extra medicine that only you could prescribe, and, believe me, it has worked wonders, not just for Sorrelle but for Gemma and Dean and now Olivia. I guess at some point these posts will come to a natural end, and I never want you to forget how you helped save a little life and, as a result, a family.

I will update again during the week. Until then, enjoy your weekends and today's caption picture.

Grandpa

10th August 2016

Caption: Really, Grandpa, you weren't allowed to watch TV in bed?! I love my mummy 😂 😊

Hi, everyone. Here we are with the latest news on Sorrelle, though there's not been much change. The adenovirus has stayed the same, which is great. Her counts are all totally fine. There is a *however* coming, though. *However* ... in typical Sorrelle style, after a fantastic week, she goes and spikes a temperature. So, she's confined to hospital. She looked a little pale yesterday and was a bit sick. Although it'll take some time for her to get better, it isn't dangerous. Remember she has beaten leukaemia, and so this is a walk in the park. More of a frustration really because in between sickness, she's playing and toddling around without a care in the world 😊

We're still hopeful she'll be discharged soon and will, of course, keep you posted. I'll update again at the weekend with the next adeno result and, hopefully, better news about the sickness.

Enjoy this gorgeous picture and have a good evening.

Grandpa

14ᵗʰ August 2016

Caption: So, you go shopping and you return with this in your bag. First thought, refund? 😊

A very good afternoon, everyone, and welcome to the latest instalment of the Sorrelle Chronicle. So, what's in the news today? Well, there's news on her numbers, the adeno, the weeks ahead – and a fun-filled hospital stayover for Grandpa!

Her immune system is measuring around 5.5, her white cells 7.7, her red blood count 139, her platelets 30 and her lymphocytes .48 (remember, this is the part of her immune system that fights the adenovirus). All these numbers are excellent apart from her platelets and lymphocytes, and this is because she's had a little sickness in the last few days and it hits the platelets first. Her tummy is also a bit swollen. This will resolve over time, and there is a small procedure they can do to help her tummy return to some sort of normality.

Now the adeno… When her lymphocytes are lower, it's because she's using them to fight the adeno. And when she's under the weather, she needs more of them to fight it. We believed there may have been a slight increase in the adeno because her tummy's swollen, and we were right. Now, please don't worry about this. The increase is from 500 to a new reading of 559. We will speak to Rob on Monday to check if this means her immune system will reduce it on its own and she's simply had a poorly week, or if there's medication that will help bring it down. The most important thing is to remember when it was dangerous it measured in the millions – now it's in the hundreds.

So, last night, lucky Grandpa here spent the night with our little hero. She basically slept all night … that is until 4am, at which point Grandpa was treated to a chorus of those wonderful noises little ones make when they're happy chattering to themselves. You parents out there will know the wonder I speak of! Those of you who haven't experienced this, my advice is to do some overnight babysitting! It took all my willpower not to burst into laughter! I remained quiet, thinking she would soon doze off, when I smelt the odour of a certain nappy. Quick as a flash, Grandpa thinks, let's change her, she will be lovely and fresh and then go back to sleep. A noble quest, I hear you say. Well, yes and no. In my attempt to be Grandpa of the Year, I had overlooked that I was to become involved in early morning playtime and a stupid o'clock viewing of Toy Story! It turns out that 4am to 5am is Sorrelle giggling time!

Now this hopefully reassures you of two things: one, she is really well in herself, and two Grandpa is – I believe the term is – knackered! Hahaha. If you ever hear these 4am noises, just go for it. Sleep, you can catch up on. The memories these little gems give you are worth every matchstick!

And so finally, the weeks ahead. Well, pretty much steady as she goes. They will look at her tummy and make a decision on the procedure, and she's still scheduled to go home soon. I expect if, and only if, they decide on speeding up her tummy issues, then home may be delayed a few days. But the medics remain delighted with her progress and they're doing all they can to discharge her as soon as they can.

Well, everyone, that's about it for today. The picture was taken today at home, where she spends the day. I hope you enjoy her remarkable smile.

As always, I will update you mid-week, when we get the next adeno result.

Take care, all.

Grandpa

19th August 2016

Caption: It's no Harley Davidson, but it's pink! 😊

Good evening, everyone, and welcome to the Sorrelle update. There have been a few developments in the last few days. I guess we start with how our little hero is in herself. As the picture from this morning shows, she is a happy little girl and taking this all in her stride. Her numbers are all very good and, after telling you the adenovirus had crept up a little, it has now reduced to 500. This is more great news because it's Sorrelle's own immune system that has reduced the adeno, not medication. We also know that the donor cells from transplant are 100%. This means there are no old Sorrelle rouge cells that can cause any problems – so the cancer is clear and her transplant perfect. This leaves us with the issues with her tummy. You'll remember me saying they had things they would try rather than let time drag on waiting for her to heal herself (while unable to process any food or drink without being sick). So, this morning, the procedure took place. Our little munchkin had a trip to theatre – not the Shakespeare kind, the hospital kind. Although she's a bit woozy and sore, she's perfectly OK and over the next few days they will try feeding into her tummy to see if the procedure has done the trick. They fully expect her tummy to work well and, after a few weeks, she'll be able to go home, where they will monitor her. Once she's completely recovered, she can look forward to a normal, happy childhood.

I will post on Monday, what will be the anniversary of Sorrelle's diagnosis. The time seems to have flown by whilst at the same time been the slowest year I've ever known. But, for today, know that she is safe, recovering, resting and smiling. And more wonderful than anything else, she is simply Sorrelle.

Have a good weekend, everyone, and I will update you all on 22nd August!

Grandpa

22nd August 2016

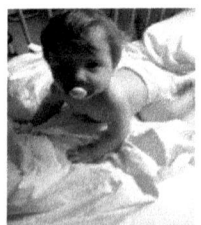

Caption: 22/8/15 to 22/8/16 – a year in the life.

Hi, everyone. So, it's almost midnight on 21st August 2015 and you receive a phone call from your daughter. You almost don't hear the words. You think you hear "suspected" and "leukaemia", but you're numb. You only know one thing – you need to be there. You don't remember dressing, driving, walking – the only thing you are aware of is the most unimaginable pain etched on your daughter's face. And the all-round disbelief. Why us? Someone's mistaken. Why Sorrelle? But is there any hope? It's only "suspected"…

And so the journey to what will become home for the next year begins. You arrive at Royal Manchester Children's Hospital and in the early hours of 22nd August 2015, your worst fears are confirmed – your daughter's daughter, this innocent ten-month-old baby has leukaemia! You make your own diagnosis based on what you think you know – that leukaemia is cancer, and cancer kills! And although you don't say the words, they're your first thought. And then you move to thoughts of your daughter, her partner and our family. How can you, in the middle of this, keep positive? How do you hold onto hope? I don't know, you just do, because you have to.

You're ushered to a "special" ward. A quiet ward where a parent walking the corridor wears a smile, where a child is helped to the toilet. You realise where you are, when a little bald head walks past you and smiles! You realise you need to snap out of it, stop feeling sorry for yourself, be strong, and wait. Yes, wait – our new four-letter word. But morning arrives and as you watch this little girl wake, that's when it hits you. She's smiling, giggling, doing all the things a happy ten-month-old does. That's right – she doesn't know what all the fuss is about. WE are the ones with the issues! And that's perfectly normal.

Then you meet the man who saves lives, Rob. He will do tests but based on what he's already seen, there's a new four-letter word – HOPE! You grasp this word with all your might and never let it go. You realise your knowledge of cancer and treatment is of another age, it took your father at 47 and so you fear the worst. And as the daylight breaks through the hospital room blinds, so does the first and most important thought – Sorrelle isn't going anywhere. She's safe, and there's a plan.

You go to the parents' room of Ward 84, where you're greeted by other parents, who carry a constant look of concern and hope. They smile, they chat, they are living what you come to realise is a new kind of normal. This is your new family – and God bless every one of them. Although you don't know it, in the months ahead you will become one of these parents greeting the latest family to hear devastating news.

And then the year begins. Nurses, doctors, medication, procedures, injections, antibiotics, tears, laughter, worry, pain, blood, platelets, chemotherapy, transplant, viruses, adeno, machines, tests, more tests, lack of sleep, friends, family, a donor, workmates, rallying round, the ward family, late night pizza. Heartbreak as little angels are taken. Delight as brave little ones leave the ward and begin a life of hope. And this is the cycle you are trapped in, repeating itself month after month. How do you cope with all this? The answer is simple. And for every family, it is just one word. For our family, that word was Sorrelle. The one common denominator in all of this is the child at the centre of it. You realise a year on that you were in some ways wrong when you said it's the adults who have the issues. Yes, we do, but Sorrelle did have issues. Well, one to be precise – cancer! And although there are hundreds of people involved, including everyone reading this post, it was Sorrelle who beat cancer. Her body said no to the clutches of this dreadful disease. Her spirit kept us filled with hope. Her determination continued as we wondered. Her heart warmed us on those cold, dark days. Yes, the children save us more than we save them.

As families, we live, we love, we hope, we dream. We have to – it's all we have. Sorrelle has beaten cancer. She has survived a bone marrow transplant made possible by an unknown hero out there. She has endured illness and pain, but – and here's the most uplifting part – she now has the chance to dream, to hope, and to grow with her sister, her mummy and her daddy into a family that has endured what no family should.

I have nothing but pride for Gemma and Dean. They've grown as people and as parents and are role models to us all. Our families, friends and workmates – you cannot imagine the difference you've made. You've been our medicine! And I can never thank you enough.

Today, Sorrelle is well. Her latest procedure will see her eating very soon. And her bone marrow is now perfect and making new blood and platelets like there's no tomorrow. The adenovirus is still at the insignificant 500 mark and her smile is there, as always.

The end of treatment bell on the ward is a symbol of hope and a future – whatever that may hold. We hope, in the not-too-distant future, Sorrelle will ring that bell and when she does, it will ring out a message to every family affected by this awful disease – a message of hope.

And so today, 22nd August 2016, a year after diagnosis, we look forward to a brighter future whilst at the same time never forgetting the journey that has defined us all. A final request from me. Please, today, contact someone you love and tell them that. Phone them, hug them, email them, Facebook them, send them a message on Twitter. Carrier pigeon them! Remember how fragile life can be. Remember family.

We were fortunate. And as I thank the heavens that Sorrelle has beaten this disease, I remember those brave little angels now dancing amongst the stars.

If you meet or talk to a family who's discovered they too are on this journey, please tell them to endure, to fight, to hope, to dream. Anything is possible!

Thank you.

Grandpa

24th August 2016

Caption: Peekaboo 😊

Good evening, all, and welcome to day 2 of year 2! The Sorrelle saga continues. Five days after her trip to theatre, she's playing peekaboo! There was a little playtime yesterday too and although she's still sore, she wants to be active. Try stopping her! I had the pleasure of the overnight shift with the little munchkin, and maybe the best example I can give you of her being sore but happy and giggly is to tell you what Sorrelle and Grandpa were doing at 3:30am! Well, she woke up, sore, and called for Mummy. Bit of a shock for her when wrinkly old Grandpa appeared from his slumber! As any doting grandpa would, I comforted her but within 30 seconds she gave me that look – the 'I don't wanna go to sleep, Grandpa' look! Let's just say I have yet to establish if the ward appreciated rousing versions (yes, plural!) of Frozen's Let It Go! It would appear our little munchkin not only has The X Factor but the whole blinkin' alphabet! Hahaha.

And so today… Her counts are all in the normal range, which, considering she had surgery five days ago, is really very good. They have begun to feed her through her gastro tube and although there have been a few teething problems, we're pretty sure this is down to her stomach getting used to food stuffs again. As tonight's caption picture shows, she's doing OK. We again begin the cycle of waiting to get her home. Oh, one final piece of good news – that dastardly adenovirus is at the base 500 figure.

So, no middle-of-the-night choruses for Grandpa tonight! I'm sure Mummy will do equally well. Sorrelle promised me she would make sure Mummy was awake! Hahaha.

My next post will have the latest adeno result, so until then, please look after yourselves. And following my anniversary post, can I take this opportunity to thank you for your kind comments. Gem and Dean read every one of them and take great comfort from them.

Grandpa

28th August 2016

Caption: Hey, Grandpa, if you stay at the hospital tonight, you'll get a kiss 😊 Oh, go on then, Munchkin, you twisted my arm!

A very good evening, everyone, and welcome to the latest news on our little hero. Once again, Grandpa got to spend the evening at hospital, which I have to say was a delight. She's not been as happy as this for a long time, and although she still has issues with her tummy, and will do for some time, she's genuinely in really good shape and in high spirits.

So, the latest numbers. White cells 8.6 – perfectly normal. Red cells 138 – amazing number and now fully self-generating. Platelets 51 – this is perfectly OK given surgery was only a week ago. And the adeno result once again is at the register figure of 500. We're going to check if this is what it will always be as there are no signs of it reducing any further.

Next week, the milk feeds will start, albeit very slowly. After so much inactivity, her stomach is very small and will fill quickly. We need to be mindful of this. She really is in great shape, though, and she was allowed home for the day today. We're edging nearer and nearer to her being discharged. Obviously, last night we had many more rousing renditions of Let It Go! I am hopeful she will soon learn another song…!

I've added a little good morning video as a special treat. After all, it's not every day a hero blows you a kiss 😊 Enjoy the rest of your weekends, everyone, and I hope you enjoy the pictures and video.

I will post again mid-week following the next adeno result.

Grandpa

SEPTEMBER 2016

1st September 2016

Caption: Sorrelle needs your help, please.

Hi, everyone. There will be my usual post tomorrow, but today I wanted to post this. Today is day one of cancer awareness for the month of September. It's not necessarily about raising money but awareness. Over the past year, you have followed Sorrelle's story and you have considerable awareness as a result. People need to know about the daily struggles of children with cancer – and the needs of the medical teams helping them. So, I am asking everyone, for the month of September, to use the gold For Kids Fighting Cancer picture as your profile picture. When your friends or family ask why, tell them about children like Sorrelle, and the little angels lost along the way. It may encourage them to use the gold picture too – which will spread awareness like ripples in a pond.

Think of it this way. There are around a hundred of you who have followed these posts. If you all used the gold picture and just one friend each asked about it, and then they too used the picture, and then one each of their friends did… I think you get the picture 😊 Think of it as a sea of gold for September and, most importantly, for awareness.

It really would mean so much to our family if you could do this – for those children who still have to fight this dreadful indiscriminate disease. Sorrelle is winning her battle, and you've all helped her do that. Now is our chance to help others.

Thanks, everyone. I look forward to seeing lots of gold.

Grandpa

2nd September 2016

Caption: Hey, Sis, I know you have to smile for your fans, but please don't drop me. I'm a little nervous here

Welcome to the latest update on Sorrelle. I hope you enjoy the caption picture today. It does seem rather apt that the sisters are together at the start of cancer awareness month, which is the reason for the other picture. If we put this into context, on 22nd August, Sorrelle was one of the 46. Over the last year, we've known seven little angels who were not so fortunate. Sorrelle is one of the 330. Now, we are able to say she is one of the survivors! That's for a lot of reasons – your support, our support, the nurses, the doctors, the donors, the research, the treatments, the funding for the research and the raising awareness.

Be under no illusion Sorrelle is here today because years ago, people wanted to know more, they spread the message, and they raised funds. The cycle can only continue if we keep telling people. I want Sorrelle's post today to be the start of our small group telling others about her so we can in time save another little Sorrelle out there. No one will ever know you did it, but every time you hear someone say that survival rates are increasing, you'll know it's because of you. I can think of no better thing to be proud of than to help destroy this terror for children and their families. Please copy the awareness picture and post it, share it, turn it into a flag and wave it if you like, but please do something with it. We sadly see and hear of terror out there almost every day and we post pictures of support by way of country flags etc. Let this cancer awareness picture be these children's flag, and please wave it as you would with other terrors.

In the latest twist, Sorrelle has started tolerating feeds into her gastro tube with no sickness! This is a massive step on the road to full recovery and the childhood we wish for her. We keep everything crossed that she will be discharged very soon.

Tonight, I'm lucky to be on night duty with the little munchkin – I'm actually looking forward to a 3am rendition of Let It Go :)

Next post will be over the weekend, when we get the next adeno result. Enjoy the picture, keep the messages coming and, together, let's make everyone out there aware of the battle.

Take care, all.

Grandpa

3rd September 2016

Caption: Grandpa shares a special treat.

Good evening, all. I like to think of myself as a sharing grandpa, who, when he says Sorrelle is doing OK, provides evidence of this. Well, feast your eyes on the pictures and videos from tonight. I told you I was lucky to be on the night shift again, and I think you'd all have to agree. She has been the happiest I've seen her since before diagnosis and she actually fell asleep giggling at me! For anyone out there who's not yet experienced the joy of children, take it from me, the best is yet to come. Even in the most testing of times, they surprise you. They laugh, they giggle, they cover you in stickers, they sing. But get them to do the one thing you long for – say 'Grandpa' – not a bl—y chance! Hahaha.

Enjoy your evenings, everyone. As you can see, tonight was one of my most enjoyable ones yet.

8th September 2016

Caption: Go on then, give us a kiss 😊

Good evening, everyone. We started the week in very high spirits. We have really good numbers and are looking to get discharged and start the home recovery chapter. As the week rolled on, Rob talked about home for the weekend – and then this morning Sorrelle decided to have her little say in the only way she knows. Yep, that's right, she spiked a 40+ temp! She's OK, but it looks like she's picked up an infection in her Hickman line, so they've put her on antibiotics. Already, her temperature has returned to normal and she's much more settled. Discharge from the hospital will now be delayed, but hopefully in a few days she'll be back on track. All other results are really good, and the adenovirus, to use Rob's words, is no longer a concern to him.

Not much more to add, other than this latest bug must be Sorrelle's way of saying she will miss the nurses! I suspect Mummy's reply would be: "Well, let's invite them home for tea then"! Gem and Dean are very used to these setbacks and, to be honest, delays are not as important as Sorrelle going home when she's well enough.

Will update you all after the weekend when we have a better idea of when the little munchkin will be going home.

Take care, all.

Grandpa

13th September 2016

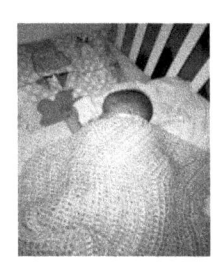

Caption: And so the small boat finally gets to sleep in her own bed!

A very good evening, everyone. It's another very special day today. 388 days after being diagnosed and officially admitted to the child oncology ward, Sorrelle "Munchkin" Turnbull was officially discharged! Yes, she is finally home, folks! Sleeping in her own bed, with her sister just a few steps away, and Mummy and Daddy just a few steps more.

We cannot begin to express just how wonderful a feeling it is. Sorrelle's numbers are totally fine and last week's hiccup's been treated. The adenovirus is hardly worth a mention. As the weeks pass, she will begin to tolerate more feeding and come off her line food. Life will then slowly but surely return to normality. The bell is getting closer.

Sorrelle now begins life as an outpatient and will attend regular clinics for a few years to check her numbers. The checks will be further apart as the months roll by. The truth is, families who go through this all too often find that leaving hospital is simply the first part of the journey. What follows are months and years of checks and tests.

But she is the best I've seen her – happy, full of mischief and as loving as ever. 388 days ago, we were unsure this day would ever come, and so we celebrate the fact it has.

I invite you to send your congrats messages to Gem and Dean and, of course, the munchkin herself. I will post again in a few days and give you a progress report following her outpatient appointment on Friday.

Take care, all.

Grandpa

16th September 2016

Caption: Breakfast, anyone? 😋

A very good morning, everyone. A quick post to tell you all is well with the little munchkin and I will be posting a full and special update tonight. There will be news on her first week at home, how recovery's going, and, if you are all good girls and boys, I may throw in the odd surprise picture or two 😊

Hope you all have a good day.

Grandpa

16th September 2016

Caption: Professor Wynn shakes the hand of the little lady he saved ♡

So, everyone, here is the treat I promised you. 391 days after being diagnosed with leukaemia, Sorrelle got to ring a very special bell! On 22nd August 2015, while Sorrelle lay in her cot having been diagnosed, I walked down the corridor to the parents' room, my mind full of disbelief and questions – and the frustration of finding no answers to those questions. I met a mum on the ward who sat and talked with me and told me about the bell and its significance: "That's the bell the children get to ring when they end their treatment and have beaten cancer." I held those words in my mind as I walked back to Sorrelle's room. I stopped and gazed at the bell and wondered if one day Sorrelle would ring it. Then I returned to my daughter, her partner, our families and there, in the cot, that innocent face smiling at everyone. Oh, little girl, if you only knew the fight you were about to start. Could we begin to comprehend the hours, weeks and months ahead? Of course we couldn't. Gem and Dean began a journey with Sorrelle that day which, despite being surrounded by family, friends and medics, was the loneliest journey they will ever endure. The devastation that hit them. The feeling of hopelessness that haunted them. The anguish etched onto their faces with every dose of chemotherapy, every needle, every visit to theatre, every antibiotic, every infection, every occasion you're told the reality of what you face, and every dark night watching the minutes tick by, knowing that each minute passed is a minute nearer to surviving that serious infection.

I've remained as positive as I can in these posts, while at the same time giving you accurate information. What you've just read is the reality that every parent on Ward 84 faces every day. Nobody's immune, and some parents have, heartbreakingly, faced the ultimate reality of this vicious and cruel disease – that they will sadly never hear that bell ring for their child. My thoughts were with every one of them today, when Sorrelle held the rope in her hand and rang that bell loud and proud. It's a noise that pierces the silence of the ward to remind us – everyone – that hope must endure, that dreams cannot end, that when you have nothing else to hold onto, you fight and fight some more.

Today, a small boat set sail once again in that big ocean. Her Fight Song, an anthem to stir us to bond as families, to inspire us. We are setting course for the future because of Professor Wynn, who never gave up; the nurses, who rallied; the donor who gave new life; the Ward 84 family, with shoulders of granite; Gemma's and Dean's families, who gave love; the army of friends and colleagues, who supported and donated.

As for your author, I hope these posts have not just informed you but encouraged you to hug that little longer, smile that little wider, and even refocus on what is truly important. Today, Sorrelle begins the next chapter of her journey, still with some recovery to make, and it's important we all remember that children who beat this disease live with the after-effects for many years.

These posts will continue a little longer, while Sorrelle fully recovers, and I will write them weekly.

I shook Rob Wynn's hand today and thanked him for saving not only my granddaughter's life but my daughter's life too. In short, he saved a family. We all did.

Thank you all for being our rocks.

Have a wonderful evening, everyone.

Grandpa

18th September 2016

Caption: A pictorial treat – my time since the bell 😊

A very good evening, everyone. I know I said it would be weekly updates, but as a special treat I thought you might like me to start the weekly posts tonight so you can see some wonderful pictures of Sorrelle since ringing the bell on Friday. She walked out of the hospital with her little cousin

Arthur to begin what can only be described as the most wonderful normality! Nights in your own bed, days out, time with family.

Sorrelle has been so very happy, and medically, there's nothing to report. I can only report on the number of smiles, giggles, mischief and her general munchkinness! And that, folks, has been just wonderful. These few days are what mean the most, and I'm sure there will be many more to share with you in the weeks ahead.

Enjoy your weekends, and I'll give you the next update on Sunday next week.

A VERY happy Grandpa.

24th September 2016

Caption: Week 1 post bellringing, and things are looking very smiley 😊

A very good morning, everyone. As promised, the first of your weekly updates on Sorrelle. As you can see from the pictures, home life seems to be agreeing with her 😊 Medically, everything is really good. Her numbers are where they should be, and her sickness is reducing every day. There are still several medicines she takes, primarily to protect her from bugs and as anti-sickness. The good news is that Gem is now slowly introducing milk feeds to her gastric tube, and she seems to be tolerating them. The big news this week is that she finally took a few bites of food orally and again tolerated them. Considering the journey she has been on, this is a big step forward. The best news for me is simply that she is happy and having a wonderful time with her sister and mummy and daddy.

I will post a short video that took her by surprise. I challenge you not to smile when you see her reaction 😂

Have a wonderful weekend, everyone.

Grandpa

OCTOBER 2016

5th October 2016

Caption: Happy days 😊

A very good afternoon, all. So, the latest instalment of the Sorrelle Gazette, with the headline 'Our hero goes from strength to strength!' Just take a look at the smiles, everyone. They say more about her condition than any words I could use. She really is the happiest we've seen her. She's now rarely sick, she's managing more feeds through her gastro tube, and she's eating more and more orally. She had her weekly check-up with Professor Wynn, who is delighted with her. She will have a routine bone marrow test at the end of October, which we are sure will show no cancer. As she recovers, they will reduce the nights spent on her chemical feeds and the medication she receives for precautionary reasons.

Sorrelle's staying over here Saturday. I very much look forward to having special Grandpa breakfast time with the little munchkin 😊 Gem, Dean and Olivia are well and very much enjoying this new family life.

My thanks to you all for your support and messages. I hope you enjoy the pictures and the sheer delight in Sorrelle's face.

See you all next week.

Take care.

Grandpa

10th October 2016

Caption: A weekend of fun.

A very good evening, everyone. I would have waited until Wednesday and the weekly hospital visit to update you on our little hero but I was watching the videos and couldn't keep them from you a moment longer!

What a wonderful weekend. I have longed for so many weeks and months to have Sorrelle here overnight and have some silly Grandpa time at breakfast. Well, finally, I got my wish, along with some time at the park. She really is progressing so well. She's eating little bits more orally every day and is tolerating her milk through her gastro tube without being sick. I am convinced her Hickman line and gastro tube will be gone in the new year, and it's clear her bowel is feeling better and better. I'm sure when she has the appointment at the end of October it will confirm steady progress. She's back to being the happy, cheeky and occasionally stubborn little girl we all know and love. But more than anything, she remains a symbol of hope. There is nothing really to report in respect of her numbers as these all continue to be normal. Being at home was, is and will be the best of all medicines.

Enjoy the videos, everyone, and do feel free not to smile if you can! Good luck with that one hahaha. On a final note, you may have seen on Sorrelle's page information about a great guy called Tom (one of my work colleagues), who, bless him, has taken it upon himself to complete a mini marathon to raise money for Sorrelle and to give her some experiences that she missed out on during her year in hospital. This is not a plea to donate, simply a very humbled grandpa taking this public opportunity to thank Tom and all of you for your selfless acts, friendship, messages of support, prayers … the list is endless. Every one of you has been just as important as any doctor or medicine in Sorrelle beating this disease and continuing with her recovery. Thank you.

Take care and see you at next week's update.

Grandpa

17th October 2016

Caption: Another weekend of fun and laughter 😊

Good evening, everyone. So, here we are, another week on and at six months free from cancer! The smile bigger than ever, the cheekiness delightful, the recovery better and better by the day. Sorrelle had a wonderful weekend with Ila and a visit from Arthur. Grandpa was a tad happy as you can imagine! 😊 Sorrelle is starting to eat even more and still the milk feeds increase. Most importantly, she's not been sick for two weeks now, and what this means is, her stomach and bowel are recovering and tolerating more. We can look forward to the chemical feeds reducing and then stopping.

Then, just when you least expect it, it's time for Sorrelle to do what Sorrelle does best – get her spanner out and throw it in the works! Yep, you guessed it – temperature! And when she spikes a temp, it's an automatic 48 hours in hospital. Please don't worry, her temperature had already started to fall when she was admitted, though they're still required to give her antibiotics and take cultures to check she doesn't have infections in her line. Pretty sure she doesn't, but because her immune system is not quite like yours or mine, she needs a boost.

But – yes, there is a but – and this is the very best example of just how well Sorrelle is. The last year has seen her need lots of antibiotics because her immune system doesn't grow when she gets a bug, unlike ours, which grows to fight an infection. That was until yesterday. Sorrelle's blood levels, platelets and immune system actually grew on their own when she got the temperature, ready to fight the infection! That's what happens when your body is working as it should! So, it's the best possible news for us that the little hero's body is doing exactly what it needs to be. So, on we go. The days are getting better and better.

On a final note, can I take this opportunity to thank Tom Goss once again for the mini marathon he completed yesterday and for contributing yet more donations to Sorrelle to experience things she missed during her illness. Tom, you are a gentleman. Thank you.

I will update again next week with what I am sure will be another week of excellent progress and lots of smiles.

Take care, all.

Grandpa

25th October 2016

Caption: I'm only stroking your arm, Sis. Please stop with the mind melt!

Good morning, everyone, and once again we find ourselves here with the Sorrelle update 😊 So, first, she has been very well. The milk feeds are increasing, as is her weight, and she's even growing a little. Her eating orally has reduced a bit, but this is because we've increased the milk to work towards getting her off the overnight chemical feeds. It's all about balance, which can be frustrating, but we are at least moving in the right direction and we're a world away from how life was after transplant. She's getting happier and cheekier by the day and we're looking forward to her second birthday on Saturday. Her numbers are all really good, and she quickly got over her little pit stop in hospital on the 17th.

And so, this last weekend, I again had the pleasure of her company, along with her little sister, which was delightful. And so to last night. Temperature over 38.5 again and, yep, you guessed it – re-admitted to hospital for cultures and antibiotics! Please try not to worry – this is normal practice for any child post-treatment to identify if there is a positive infection. If the cultures come back positive, then she has five days of antibiotics in hospital before she can be considered for discharge. We expect the culture results later today and if they're negative, she'll be home in a couple of days, in time for her birthday. If not, then it could well be a second birthday on the ward, but in honesty that's just geography! The most important thing is she's relatively well and not in any danger at all.

I'd just like to make a final mention about Tom Goss. I wanted to say here on Sorrelle's page a huge thank you to Tom, not just for raising the money but, more importantly, for the generosity of spirit he's showed. It's the Toms of this world who make these journeys children find themselves on more bearable, as indeed do you all with your donations, good wishes, and messages of support and love.

I will update again nearer to the little munchkin's birthday. For now, take care, all.

Grandpa

29th October 2016

Caption: A very special day.

A very good morning, everyone. This is not the weekly update. That will be posted on Sunday.

This is simply a grandpa wishing a rather special granddaughter a very happy 2nd birthday. This little girl has shown courage and spirit beyond her tender years. She has inspired us all and taught us, without speaking a word, the importance of love and family. You may all know of a famous poem called "If". When I think of Sorrelle, I am reminded of a few words from one line in that poem: "If you can keep your head, when all about you are losing theirs."

That is exactly what Sorrelle did. When we were unsure, frightened, sad, angry or frustrated, Sorrelle just kept on being Sorrelle, fighting her way through cancer, transplant and life-threatening viruses. She astounded the medical teams. And I know that had her illness struck me, I would not have been as brave and courageous as this little girl.

And so, if you will, please forgive this soft old grandpa for using this update site with no update, to publicly express my love for this special little girl, to thank her for this past year and for making me a better person, and to wish her a beautiful day with her mummy, daddy and sister xxx

Update on Sunday everyone.

Take care.

Grandpa

30th October 2016

Caption: Birthday girl – the update.

Good evening, everyone, and welcome to the latest update on our little hero. As you know, Sorrelle was re-admitted to hospital on Monday with a high temperature. She hasn't had a high temp since, though cultures taken from her line do show an infection. She seems to be keeping it at bay with antibiotics and her immune system. Her white cells and platelets are totally fine and although she had a tiny bit of sickness once a few days ago, that is the only time over the past month. So, things are pretty good, and we're hoping over the next week plans can be put in place to get her lines out once and for all, and for her bowel to fully recover and begin working. I would guess that'll take us into the new year, but at this point we would like to think that she can finally begin to eat as we do. Still a little way to go, but she's laughing, speaking, walking and enjoying doing more of the little things children do.

And so to her birthday yesterday. Sorrelle had a wonderful day with her family. I'm sure you'll have seen more pictures of the day from Gemma. For me, the one of her with Gem, Dean and Olivia says it all. Can I thank all of you for your birthday messages, cards and gifts. You made what was a special day even more special.

I would like to take a moment of your time and ask a small favour. Last year, Sorrelle was joined on Ward 84 by a little girl called Jessica and her mum and dad, Nikki and Andy. This beautiful little girl is four years old, and two weeks ago, Nikki and Andy were handed the news no parent wants or deserves to hear. Jessica is slipping away and has only a few more weeks with her mummy, daddy and baby brother, James. We had the privilege of seeing Jessica today with her parents and friends. Nikki and Andy are loving parents, with a dignity that speaks volumes. I would like you all, please, to spare a moment tonight to close your eyes and send your thoughts to this lovely family and very special little girl.

Thank you, everyone. Another update for you next week.

Take care.

Grandpa

NOVEMBER 2016

7th November 2016

Caption: Go on then, Daddy, you can live in my house!

A very warm welcome to this week's update on the mighty Sorrelle. As you can see, she is back at home – her very own little home hahaha. As you all know, she was admitted back on the ward a couple of weeks ago after spiking a temperature and, in typical Sorrelle style, she hasn't spiked a temperature since! There was, however, a nasty bug in her line and so last week they had to remove the line and put in another one. All pretty routine, but it did mean that the chemical feeds missed a couple of days, which meant her calcium level dropped and she had to stay in hospital. You'll be delighted to know that's been corrected, and she was discharged today and she's back to being a weekly outpatient. She's steadily improving day by day and the medical team are delighted with her progress. It was, of course, frustrating having to celebrate her second birthday in hospital, but Sorrelle just sees the people and presents – the rest is geography! Her bloods today gave good results, and we continue with building her feeds and moving towards her gastro tube and Hickman line being removed in the weeks/months ahead. She is as cheeky as ever and is loving life. Seeing Sorrelle and those gorgeous little cousins of hers is all this grandpa needed for his birthday, that's for sure 😊

Hope you enjoy the caption pictures tonight. I have to say it's almost impossible not to smile when you look at them!

Have a great evening, everyone.

Grandpa

14ᵗʰ November 2016

Caption: Ingredients – one little girl, one Peppa Pig trampoline, one smile. Mix together, leave to play, and the result ... happy!

A very good evening to you all and welcome once again to the latest post featuring our little hero 😊 You will all be happy to know Sorrelle is back at home. It was pretty frustrating having her in there for two weeks, especially when she didn't spike a temperature the whole period she was in! But these protocols have a purpose, and it's much better to know she's safe. Now we're continuing with her recovery, eating, and milk intake so the chemical feed can be reduced – and hopefully end – in the weeks ahead. The issue with her bowel is also cause for good news, in that there are real signs of major improvement, so much so they're scheduling the procedure to reverse her stoma in the next few weeks. At the last outpatient appointment on Wednesday, Professor Wynn finally used the two words he always said he never would: "It's gone"! These mean everything, coming from him. Following the latest screening of Sorrelle's bone marrow, he's now confident to say the cancer has gone! This is very different to him saying there are no signs, which leaves room for doubt and further checks. For him to say it's gone gives Gem and Dean that reassurance that the battle against this cruel disease has come to an end and has been won. Now comes the recovery, not from the disease but from the 14 months of treatment and chemicals her body's been subjected to.

Sorrelle is happy and well. She's talking more every day, and that cheeky, playful personality that served her so well in her battle continues to warm our hearts daily.

I will update again next week. Until then, take care. Thank you for your support and messages.

Grandpa

21st November 2016

Caption: Day 454 and still a pretty happy Grandpa 😊

Good evening, everyone, and welcome to the latest update on Sorrelle. As I am sure you can see from the picture, the little munchkin continues to smile her way back to full health. Medically, there is nothing to report. Her counts remain good and there have been no spikes in temperature, which, of course, means no hospital 😊 In a few weeks she will have a small procedure to check the recovery of her bowel and if that looks better, then in the new year, she will probably have the procedure to reverse the stoma. I have to say, every day she seems stronger, happier, cheekier and healthier. The road has been long, and there is still a little way to go. But, as a family, we are so very fortunate that Sorrelle has survived everything this dreadful disease has thrown at her. To everyone out there, huge thanks for the part you have played in Sorrelle's fight and recovery.

You seasoned readers will know I have asked small favours of you on occasion. Tonight, I need your help again. You will recall a very special young lady called Alison recently losing her fight and me asking you to keep her family in your thoughts. Today, the final farewells were said. I would ask you all to please hold Alison and her family in your thoughts. As if this awful disease had not claimed enough innocent lives, I also have to tell you that Jessica, the little girl I mentioned two weeks ago, lost her battle yesterday. She was a very special little girl, and we will all miss her beautiful smile. Gem and Dean have become close friends with so many families, and it has been a time of real contrast as they celebrate Sorrelle's recovery yet have to say goodbye to so many sweet children.

You may have seen there is a petition to force the government to debate childhood cancer, and I would kindly suggest you add your name to it. It'll be one of the most worthwhile five minutes you will ever spend in your life.

From a very humble grandpa, thank you.

28th November 2016

Caption: Just giggle like me, Sis. It works every time 😊

A very good evening, everyone. It's time for the latest Sorrelle update. She's happy, smiling, no temperature 😊 Our little munchkin gets stronger every day she spends at home. It's increasingly obvious that being at home is the medicine she needs.

Last Wednesday, Professor Wynn again remarked how delighted he is with Sorrelle's progress. A little weight loss, but he's not worried – she still wants to eat, and the chemical feeds are giving her body the goodness it requires. We're scheduled for a December procedure, which will begin the process for the stoma reversal. Tomorrow, she gets to spend the day celebrating her mummy's birthday. She's really looking forward to Christmas, and I'm sure she will sail through the procedure in the same way she has her treatment.

I will next update after the procedure, which is on 5th December.

Thank you for the messages of support.

Take care, all.

Grandpa

DECEMBER 2016

4th December 2016

Caption: Not far to the finish line now, Grandpa 😊

A very good evening to you all and welcome to our update on the little munchkin. As you can see from the picture, she is in really good shape and continues to enjoy being out of hospital. No temps since her last hospital stay, so let's hope we get a clear run through Christmas. Last Wednesday's clinic was very good indeed. She is generating her own red cell count, her platelets are normal, and her white cell count is 7, which again is great. And her immune system is in really good shape. Tomorrow, she's having a procedure to check how well her bowel is recovering. This will give us an idea of when they can look at reversing her stoma, which, in turn, will determine for how much longer she'll have chemical feeds via her Hickman line and meds through her gastro tube. As I've said before, when we get into the new year we'll be a lot closer to seeing her – to use a modern term – "wireless"! It's been a long journey, littered with ups and downs. All we can do is hope we now have only ups ahead.

If you've been touched by this dreadful disease, cancer, you'll know it never leaves your thoughts. Despite every fibre of my being hoping everything will stay well, no matter how positive I am, I've asked myself, what if this is life for Gem and Dean? I want to repeat how proud this grandpa is of them both, given their reality. I am only the parent of a parent of a cancer survivor and, thankfully, I have not had to endure the torment of my child facing this indiscriminate disease.

We have lost some beautiful children, and I want to extend my deepest and sincerest wishes to the parents coming to terms with the worst thing imaginable. I hope you find some form of peace amidst your torment. You have my sincere admiration. Please spare a moment for those beautiful children I have told you about and their heroic parents.

I remain thankful that this little girl will enjoy this Christmas, and that morning I will take a moment, glance upward and think of those extra angels.

Take care, everyone. See you at the next weekly update.

Grandpa

11th December 2016

Caption: Well, at least when I'm in hospital I have a range of hat wear, Grandpa

☺

A very good evening, everyone, and welcome to this week's update on the progress of our little hero. As you may have gathered from the caption, she's back in hospital! She's had cultures done and has begun antibiotics, which should end around Wednesday. As long as the infection's gone, she'll be allowed home, just in time for Christmas. She's got a horrible bug in her Hickman line. However, as the picture shows, she's very well in spite of it. Comforting to know that the bug she has is a new one to the doctors! Isn't that just The Sorrelle Way! Thankfully, Microbiology are aware of it and know which antibiotics are especially effective in getting rid of it. Aside from this hiccup, Sorrelle is recovering. There will be a secondary test on her bowel soon so we can schedule treatment to resolve this once and for all. I will keep you posted on this in the weeks ahead. Her counts are good and she's not had a temperature since she was admitted.

Once again, thank you for your support, for the messages to Gem and Dean, and for your continued interest in Sorrelle's fight. You are all very special people and make such a positive difference not just to Sorrelle but to Gem, Dean and Olivia. Your comments give them comfort, and it's especially nice for them that you realise the fight doesn't stop after the last chemotherapy but goes on for months and years. So, from a very grateful grandpa, thank you so much.

Have a lovely evening, all.

Grandpa

18th December 2016

Caption: So, Sorrelle, do you know how to make a Swiss Roll?

Of course, Daddy. Push him down a hill! 😂

A very good evening, everyone, and welcome to the weekly update on Sorrelle's progress. You'll be delighted to know Sorrelle brushed aside the bug and is back home. In typical Sorrelle fashion, she kept us on a knife edge as to whether she'd be home for Christmas, but as long as there are no more temperatures, she can recover at home. Now to keep everything crossed that in a week's time she'll be able to enjoy a much-deserved family Christmas with Mummy, Daddy and sister.

Her numbers are where they need to be, and the very best news is that Sorrelle is finally beginning to eat more normally. For the first time in months, she's had breakfast, and she's starting to feel hungry at the right times, which, of course, means her food intake's increasing. This will greatly help the prognosis in respect of her chemical feeds. Once we get into the new year the medical team will begin to resolve Sorrelle's other issues.

Thank you all for your messages to Gem and Dean during these recent medical hiccups. They really do help them. And so on to Christmas week. This will be my last post before Christmas Eve, and I would like to close by wishing you all a happy and peaceful Christmas. To those families who are preparing for a Christmas without their beautiful and inspirational children whom we had the privilege to know – I cannot imagine your anguish. You are in our thoughts and our hearts. When the Christmas hour dawns, I will think first of those beautiful angels. Could I please ask you to remember the amazing children who won't be with us. And those of us who are fortunate to be around our families, please hug them a little tighter, give them an extra kiss, laugh with them a little longer and love them a little more publicly. We don't realise how fragile life is and how short it can be until it is too late. This is one grandpa who over the past 16 months has realised only too well what is important.

Take care, everyone, and have a peaceful Christmas.

Grandpa

24th December 2016

Hey, Grandpa, one year on and I have more hair – and you have more circumference! ☺

Good evening to all my family and friends. So, here, you see two pictures, one from last Christmas Eve and one from today. I said last year how important time with family is and just how much we take for granted. Thanks to amazingly talented doctors and nurses, our incredible NHS, a wonderful anonymous lady who donated bone marrow and you, our army of family and friends, with your love and support this Christmas, Sorrelle is cancer-free, with a very good prognosis. I took notice of my own message last year and focused on what was important and tried to maximise every moment with those I love. It has been an emotional, humbling journey. While 2017 has a really positive outlook for Sorrelle, I remember those beautiful children who will be missing Christmas, and the unimaginable time their wonderful, brave parents will have to endure. Their 2017 will be full of heartbreaking anniversaries. I would like to extend my heartfelt thoughts to those parents and pray they are able to find some peace. I will always remember their children's smiles and bravery.

As you prepare for your Christmas Day, please think of those angels now watching us and remind yourselves just how fortunate we are to be sharing these family times. Let 2017 be a year of reflection on what we can do better, a chance to spend more family time together, and a time to find peace and the strength to endure.

Merry Christmas to you all, from a very fortunate grandpa.

27th December 2016

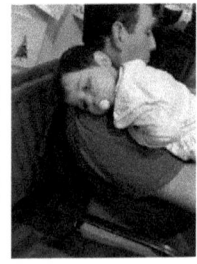

Caption: Merry Christmas, everyone. Awake, then asleep ☺

A very good afternoon to you all. I hope you are having a good Christmas. Our little hero had a wonderful Christmas – thankfully with no temperatures. She did leave it until the last minute to be discharged, but we got there in the end. The last post had her at home but then, in rather typical Sorrelle fashion, she spiked a temperature and had to be re-admitted. However, last Thursday, she was well enough to come home and since then the little lady has been partying! I cannot convey my delight in having her home and watching Gemma and Dean enjoy a family Christmas together with the girls. Sorrelle goes back to clinic tomorrow for her outpatient appointment, where I am sure they will find her well. We now look forward to the new year and her ongoing recovery. I will update you all next week, or should that be next *year*.

I would like to close this year's posts with three very important messages. To those parents who became our friends during Sorrelle's time on Ward 84 and have had to endure their first Christmas with an empty chair – you are in our thoughts, as are your beautiful, brave angels, whom we will never forget. To all of you who have supported Gem and Dean in so many ways, please accept my heartfelt thanks. Without your support, this journey, I'm sure, would have been even more unbearable.

Finally, as we end 2016, please remind your friends, and friends of friends, that child cancer doesn't stop. It doesn't take Christmas off or decide that there won't be any children diagnosed in 2017. This battle goes on. I for one will keep asking myself one simple question – what can I do to help this cruel, indiscriminate disease end? Let's all ask ourselves that question and then maybe, just maybe, one Christmas in the future, we can say we helped more families experience what we have this Christmas – a Christmas cancer-free, a new year full of new dreams, and a family saved.

I hope 2017 brings you happiness, health and strength. Take care, everyone, and Happy New Year.

Grandpa

2017

JANUARY 2017

3rd January 2017

Caption: New year, new beginning. Erm, no – back in hospital again!

A very good afternoon, everyone, and a very happy new year. As you can see, Sorrelle managed to party her way through Christmas and New Year – before the partying came to an abrupt end on Sunday, when, in unmistakable Sorrelle fashion, she spiked a temperature and became a guest of Royal Manchester Children's Hospital once more. She hasn't spiked since being admitted, and it would appear the visit will be a pretty short one. Her numbers are perfectly fine. This year should be the year when the final elements of Sorrelle's recovery are in place, and she can finally regain the childhood she's missed out on. I'll continue to keep you updated on a weekly basis.

Take care, all.

Grandpa

11th January 2017

Caption: Driving Little Miss Daisy ☺

Good evening, all. Here we are with a report on the little marvel that is Sorrelle. The good news is that she's managed to stay out of hospital! Thought we all deserved a treat, so this evening there's a caption video instead of a picture. I have to say, she is looking happier every day, which is truly heartwarming.

So, on to the second piece of good news… Professor Wynn checked her transplant figures and she remains 100% donor. There's no sign of any of the rogue cells that caused the leukaemia. All her obs are excellent, and there are no concerns, which brings me to the final piece of good news.

The initial procedure on her bowel was done on Monday, and the results indicate that Sorrelle has a good chance of full recovery with no lasting issues. Our little warrior is getting closer to closing this difficult chapter of her young life. It is, of course, difficult to put a time frame on no more wires and a recovered bowel, but I'd say it'll be another four or five months. A day at a time will do nicely. Be assured Sorrelle is in really good shape.

Enjoy the video and I will catch up next week.

Grandpa

19th January 2017

Caption: Hey, Dad, look at this. I think I've found the light at the end of that tunnel!

A very good morning to you all. How about a little update to start our day? Yesterday, Sorrelle had her latest outpatient visit. As most of you will know, she had significant damage to her bowel following the chemicals and treatment she had, which meant having a stoma and colostomy bag while her bowel tried to recover. The investigation has been to establish how blocked her bowel is, how surgery might correct it, and if she would be left needing a colostomy bag for life. I am happy to report they've concluded that a small operation will resolve any remaining issues and they're confident they can reverse the stoma. Once this is done, they can start to reduce the chemical feeds, remove the Hickman line, then remove the gastro tube and, finally, after a long journey, Sorrelle will continue her childhood wireless! Four to five months seems to be a pretty accurate time frame.

Of course, we all know Sorrelle being Sorrelle will throw a spanner in the works, but it'll only be the odd bug and temperature. We really are getting close to the day when normal service will resume. The medics are very pleased with her and still as in love with her as ever. The most pleasing thing for me is not only Sorrelle's wonderful smile but seeing Gem and Dean smiling too – smiles that show excitement for the future.

Have a great day, everyone, and I will update you next week.

Grandpa

26th January 2017

Caption: Mummy, we need to talk about this "earning your keep" idea of yours!

A very good evening, everyone, and welcome to the weekly update on Sorrelle's progress. Yesterday she attended her hospital appointment with Professor Rob Wynn (medical magician). To say he is happy with her progress is an understatement. He is delighted! The blockages in her bowel are all but gone, and all that remains is a little scar tissue, which is a result of the chemicals her body has had to absorb. The good news is that the small op she needs to reverse the stoma will include cleaning up the scar tissue so that she can function more normally. He's confident they'll then be able to remove her Hickman line and gastro tube quite quickly. The most significant event at the appointment was the moment our little hero turned to Rob and said in her sweet little way "Bob hug", at which point Rob sank to his knees and cuddled his star patient. Gemma tells me they were close to tears!

In short, Sorrelle's getting better every day. Her height and weight are increasing, and she's a sweet but cheeky little girl. Kind of like her mum – minus the sweet! Seriously, though, we're seeing more and more normality, which, of course, is the real sign of just how well she is.

It's some time since I've told you about blood counts and platelets – and with good reason. Nothing to report! We're only a few short months away from the prize and the joy of watching Sorrelle enjoy everything a little girl should. We're expecting the procedure to be done by the end of February, but I will let you know when.

Thank you for your continued support to Gemma, Dean and the girls. It warms them to see you all still sharing Sorrelle's news, and they are immensely grateful.

Have a good evening, all.

Grandpa

26th January 2017

Caption: A little extra… Oh, Mummy and Daddy, if you only knew the mischief we're going to get up to 😊

FEBRUARY 2017

1st February 2017

Caption: So, Grandpa, that's the sugar and spice. I must be the all things nice ☺

A very good evening, everyone, and welcome to the hot-off-the-press news about our little hero. Well, today being Wednesday meant the weekly visit to hospital. The news is once again really good. After another week at home eating more – and enjoying eating – it came as no great surprise that Sorrelle's put on weight. No concern with her blood tests. Sorrelle is recovering very well indeed. There were many times when we worried about her laboured recovery, but it seems it's picking up momentum by the day, rather than decreasing. She's happy – with a large portion of cheekiness thrown in! And, most importantly, she makes Gem and Dean smile every day. In those dark days, it was hard to know if there would be daily smiles, but anguish has given way to hope, tears to smiles and day-to-day endurance to dreams.

I did promise you all news of the bowel procedure and we did today receive word it's scheduled for the beginning of March. Once this is done, we would expect Sorrelle to recover over a week or so and then they'll start the process of reducing and removing chemical feeding and the Hickman line, followed by the gastro tube. And then – the simplest of actions we take for granted – the chance to pick up Sorrelle and cuddle her tight, without worrying about moving a tube or having to hug her with a safe gap. The last time this grandpa cuddled the little munchkin with no wires was 16th August 2015. The chance to hug her free from wires fills me with joy, and I'm sure it'll be the moment when, for me, this chapter draws to a close and a new one begins. I suspect it will be quite a moment.

Gemma and Dean were told today that Sorrelle is so well there's no need to attend clinic next week and so the next visit will be in two weeks' time. I will post a short update next week and then the following week, by which time I'm sure we'll have confirmation of the procedure date. Until then, thank you all once again for your messages and support and for following the little munchkin's progress.

Take care.

Grandpa

2nd February 2017

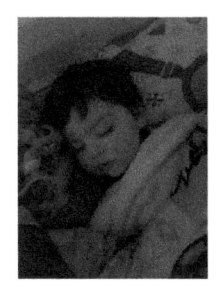

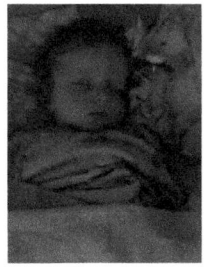

Caption: A little extra... Sleeping beauties 😊   *A grandpa's heart melts* 💜

3rd February 2017

Caption: Cheers, Grandpa, and welcome back to hospital!

Good evening, everyone. Yes, you guessed it. Last night, as Gemma and Dean looked forward to a first weekend away in some time, a certain little girl decided to spike a temperature! And so once more unto the ward, dear friends, once more! And so, whilst Gem and Dean try to enjoy a mini break in Holland, Grandpa and Sorrelle will keep the hospital busy! It's just a heavy cold, but the protocol insists that she stays in for 48 hours while cultures are taken to ensure there are no line infections. We've been here many times before. So, Gem and Dean – who I am sure will be reading this – don't worry and have fun. Munchie is just fine.

Have a good evening, all.

Grandpa

12th February 2017

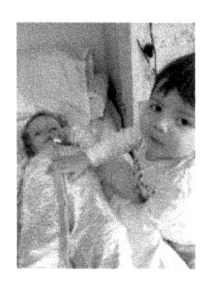

Caption: In this together, Sis.

Good evening, everyone. It's been a while since the last update. And in true Sorrelle style, she's been pretty busy! It's been a kinda in and out week – in and out of hospital, that is! Last weekend, as you all know, Sorrelle was admitted with a high temperature, but was able to return home Saturday night. Unfortunately, the bug didn't completely go and she was admitted again. She has an infection in her line and will need a fair few days of antibiotics to get rid of it. On a positive note, she's well and her improvement will stand her in good stead for her stoma reversal. We're confident that if all goes well with that, then her Hickman line can be removed quite quickly. And that, of course, means no further trips to hospital if her temperature spikes.

I will update later in the week and let you know once Sorrelle has been discharged.

Take care, all.

Grandpa

19th February 2017

Caption: Hey, look, Grandpa – three dummies! ☺

Hi, everyone, and welcome to the latest update on Sorrelle. She has finally been discharged, following a week or so of flu and E. coli. She's back to her cheeky self and her temp is normal. She's still scheduled for the stoma reversal on 3rd March and so, to be on the safe side, she will return to hospital a few days before surgery. They'll monitor her temp and make sure she doesn't spike and therefore delay any surgery. After her surgery, there'll be a short recovery period, and then the removing of her lines will begin.

Not a long update this time. Simply to let you know she's back in good shape. I will update again just before the surgery and then obviously once surgery is complete. Please keep the messages of support coming for Gem and Dean. We're getting nearer to that light at the end of the tunnel.

Take care, all.

Grandpa

MARCH 2017

2nd March 2017

So, nursey, this is the plan – little op tomorrow and let's lose the stoma bag ☺

Hi, everyone. Welcome to the news on the little munchkin. As you all know, she was in hospital last week with a temperature. Rather than discharge her, they felt keeping her in prior to her procedure would help regulate her health and ensure the operation went ahead. And so, here we are, folks, the day before the start of the final treatment journey. At 9am tomorrow, Sorrelle is scheduled to have her stoma reversed. This is an important day, a vital step towards removing the Hickman line and gastro tube.

After what seems an age, Sorrelle will be able to play and rough around without the worry of her stoma getting sore or infected. Gem and Dean are both nervous and happy for this step to finally be here. It will be some time after lunch when we know how successful the procedure was. We will, of course, let you know as soon as we do. Tomorrow will be an emotional reminder of how her bravery, courage and spirit helped her beat a vicious disease that came far too close to the abyss.

Please, if you get a moment, send your thoughts to Gem and Dean and join me in sending a very brave little girl our love for a successful morning and a speedy recovery.

Take care, all.

Grandpa

3rd March 2017

Grandpa is watching over you even more today, Munchkin. I love you so very much, little partner ♡ xx

3rd March 2017

Hi, all. Just a quick update to let you know that the little munchkin is back from her procedure, well and very sleepy. I will update tomorrow, but for now she is OK and resting. Thank you all for your good wishes.

Grandpa

4th March 2017

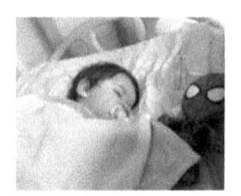

Caption: While a superhero sleeps, a soft toy watches over ☺

A very good morning, all. As promised, a little more of an update on Sorrelle. Unless we have any returning visitors from Mars this morning, I think we were all aware of Sorrelle's procedure yesterday. For a nail-biting five hours, we waited while, once again, skilled surgeons provided the little munchkin with the medical support to continue her remarkable road towards the end of her battle with leukaemia and the assorted complications along the way. We have marvelled at her bravery, resilience and sunny disposition throughout and been in awe of the care and skill of the professor and the many doctors, nurses and surgeons.

Yesterday, that small boat we all love so much continued her voyage and became stoma-FREE! The surgeons reassured Gem and Dean that it went really well and although, in typical Sorrelle style, extra work was needed, the reversal is fully complete. She is heavily sedated and receiving pain relief and that will continue for a while. She's not to eat or drink until Monday to allow her bowel to settle. Last night Gemma told me Sorrelle managed a little laugh, which, she discovered, hurts. And here is why this child has become so loved. Despite the discomfort, she continued to laugh, providing her mummy and daddy with much-needed reassurance that all is well. Of course, medical teams reassure you but there's nothing quite like the giggle of a child to ease your worries. And so now, as she recovers, we ready ourselves for the final treatment, which, as I have said, should follow in a matter of weeks.

While this very nervous and emotional grandpa waited from afar for the news on Sorrelle, I reflected on the emotions Gem and Dean have been through and I came to two conclusions. First, they have a remarkable daughter (well, two actually) and second, what great role models they are for all parents out there. This very humbled and proud grandpa is so thankful that Sorrelle was born to such amazing parents.

I will update you all in a few days, to allow for Sorrelle's recovery. My sincere thanks for your good wishes and support. These are the very moments when they're appreciated the most.

Take care.

Grandpa

5th March 2017

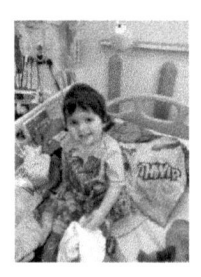

Caption: All well in the world of Sorrelle.

Hello, everyone. No big update today. Just thought you might like to see what two days post-op looks like! It would appear no one told Sorrelle that surgery takes it out of you! Hahaha. She's doing well, but she does get a little sore. And after her sitting-up episode, she was sore for a while, as you can imagine. The doctors are delighted with her progress, and we're hoping that over the next few days her bowel will wake up and start to function. After months of no use, it really does kind of go to sleep. Now the procedure has been done, her bowel will recognise it needs to start working.

Will give it a week or so and then send you another update. As always, thank you for your messages and support.

Grandpa

12th March 2017

Caption: Yes, Grandpa, I loved our playtime 4am to 6am, but forgive me if I now sleep at 10am! 😂😂

Time for an update. So, we are just over a week following Sorrelle's stoma reversal. The biggest question has to be, has it worked? Well, so far so good. I'll spare you the detail, but her bowel is starting to function and as each day passes, it appears a little more normal. You have to bear in mind it was major surgery and so healing and function will take time. And it's important not to rush things – despite Sorrelle's playful, party attitude in the early hours! Oh, the youth of today!

Her calcium levels are a bit of a nuisance and are fluctuating, part due to the surgery and part due to a possible underlying issue. They're looking into this. The only relevance this has right now is in the little munchkin having to remain in hospital until her calcium shows stable readings at the right level for at least 48 hours. Obviously, we hope this will happen in the next few days and she can go home – though, given how far we've come, a few more days or weeks is nothing. Once this is resolved, she'll be able to start eating more and retaining the nutrients she needs. And then next on the list will be the Hickman line removal. This is probably a few weeks away but certainly within sight. Finally, it'll be the gastro tube removal and then she'll be pretty much done. In short, we are getting closer to the prize every day.

Grandpa, however, is knackered, thanks to the little lady animal! Let's not tell anyone that, actually, I had the time of my life. There's nothing quite like cuddling up on a hospital bed watching princesses on TV, breaking out the occasional giggle as she tries to share her dummy with me and insists I need a new nappy! Special times with a very inspirational little girl.

So, home for Grandpa. Nana and then Mummy and Daddy to take over. Update done, now to rest. Will update again soon, everyone.

Take care.

Grandpa

23rd March 2017

Caption: One of us was 30 on Tuesday ☺ Guess which one!

A very good evening, everyone, and time for the Sorrelle news. It's been a kind of hokey cokey week! In out, in out – of hospital! Once her bowel started to work, it caused nappy rash, which has been pretty sore for her, and an infection's meant her temperature's been nudging up. So, to make her comfortable, they decided to admit her. She's on an antibiotic cream and is on the mend. She's grown and her weight's normal. She's eating and is on her way to having a day or so without PN, which gets us nearer to removing the Hickman line. She's smiling up a storm. Her immune system's dropped sharply in her blood, but this is due to it focusing on areas of her body that need it. I'm sure in the next few weeks she will take that next step to a normal childhood. In the meantime, lucky Daddy got to spend his special birthday in hospital with the little munchkin and, of course, Olivia and Gem.

On a final note, Grandpa would like to wish this young man a very happy 30th birthday and tell him publicly how proud we are of him and the courage he has shown on his own journey. He has dug deep on many occasions to support Gemma and the girls through this ordeal, despite his own medical difficulties. I, for one, as Gemma's dad and the girls' grandpa, want to thank you, Dean, for being a caring and reliable rock for Gemma – and a wonderful father.

Another update next week. In the meantime, thank you for your messages and support. Take care, all.

Grandpa

APRIL 2017

1st April 2017

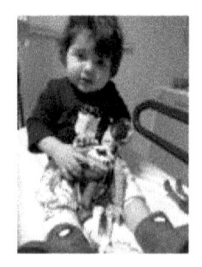

Caption: Celebrating transplant's 1st birthday the only way I know – in hospital!

A very good evening, or should that be a very good early morning! So, a year after transplant, and on the day Gemma and Dean take a couple of nights' break, Sorrelle, in keeping with her time-honoured tradition, spikes a temperature and winds up in hospital again. Cue Grandpa for hospital duty, Grandma for Olivia duty, and the break goes ahead. The Grandparent Express will be calling at Granny's and Nanna's tomorrow!

So, an update then. Yep, she's fine! Temp is now lower and, yes, she has a bit of a cold and is still recovering from the stoma reversal, but all in all, she's in pretty good shape. And how do I know this, I hear you ask. Let's try Cinderella, biscuits, milk, pretzel sticks and Baa Baa Black Sheep at 2am! Along with giggles! That's right, Grandpa, it's party time! So, despite a hospital stay, once again our little hero is in good spirits. The never-ending recovery will come to a conclusion soon and, in saying that, we're now experimenting with a couple of nights without the chemical feeds to see if her body's retaining nutrients. If her blood results show she is, then we'll be heading towards no more nights wired up and removing her Hickman line.

Quite a way to celebrate her 1st transplant birthday. It's worth a pause to send this family's heartfelt thanks to a lady we don't know for the gift of bone marrow and saving this very special little girl. Look closely at today's picture and that smile filled with a zest for life and a wonderful future – the desperately hard days and nights when we were told to prepare for the unimaginable seem a lifetime ago.

On this special day, another round of thanks to the remarkable medical teams providing the very best of care during Sorrelle's recovery. Thanks to family and friends for your support, love and understanding. You make such a difference, and Gemma and Dean could not have got through this without you.

Another update next week. For now, shhh – I think she's finally asleep!

Good night, all.

Grandpa

9th April 2017

Caption: Everyone else gets an engine!

A very good afternoon, everyone, and welcome to a Sorrelle Sunday snapshot. First news – she's back in hospital! Yep, temp over 38 and so she was admitted yesterday. This time, however, she's done it properly and has a line infection. This means a hospital stay for at least five days and antibiotics to shift the bug. Now that, my friends, is the bad news finished. And so to the good news…

Her height and weight are great, she's eating more by the day and her bowel is working better too. It's started to retain nutrients for longer, especially calcium, which you might remember is the reason her PN (wired feeds) are continuing every night. Well, the great news is this has now been reduced to give her two nights per week off lines. And next week, the hope is to go to every other day off lines. Given she has an infection in her line, they may just choose to remove it and not replace it. Will have to wait and see. We've been told they'll remove her gastro tube (to her tummy) at the same time. This is really great news and means we're no more than a month from the little munchkin being "wireless" – quite apt in today's digital world! Haha. Of course, it also means we're closer to the day when all treatment has completely finished and she moves to quarterly checks. She'll stay on the hospital's radar for five years, at which point the hospital would consider her no more likely to get cancer again than anyone else.

As Sorrelle ends her treatment and her lines are removed, I'll compile one final post before slipping into the shadows. From that moment, Gem and Dean, I'm sure, will post family pictures and catch-ups to show you how Sorrelle is doing.

o that's the post for this week. I will update again next week. Have a good evening, all.

Grandpa

15th April 2017

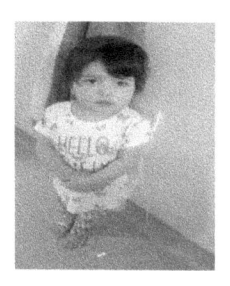

Caption: The Sorrelle challenge. Look at the picture without saying ahhh 😊

A very good morning, everyone, and welcome on this fine Easter Saturday to the Sorrelle update. Thought I'd get this in before the Easter Bunny arrives and we're all knee deep in chocolate!

I have good news and not-so-good news. Sorrelle's still in hospital, and it was indeed a pretty nasty bug in her line. It's meant a week of antibiotics. Her calcium has fluctuated – initially, steadily and over the last couple of days, dropping a little. So, now for the better news. She has been off line feeds (PN) for five days and her weight is spot on for her height. Of course, the more she eats, the better, but the point here is that she hasn't needed the PN to keep her weight. The PN is just for calcium. When Rob came in a couple of days ago, he assured us he doesn't want Sorrelle on PN for this purpose and so she's going on the list to have the line removed! We're hopeful this will happen in the next couple of days. The low calcium will be resolved through a Vitamin D supplement.

Other news… Her bowel is working better every day, the soreness has all but gone and her angelic nature is plain for all to see. I have to say it's starting to get very exciting and, of course, the nerves are jangling at the thought of flying solo, as it were, but hey, let's remember where we all were on 22nd August 2015! The journey's almost complete. Wireless status is almost here, as is a future for this little girl.

Have a wonderful Easter with your families and please pause with me and remember those brave little souls whose mums and dads face another tormenting time. This vicious indiscriminate disease has taken the families' happiness and replaced it with emptiness. My heart goes out to each and every one of you.

Take care.

Grandpa

16th April 2017

Caption: Easter Sunday with a Sorrelle twist…

A very good evening to you all and welcome to an extra and pretty special update on the little munchkin. You may remember me telling you that we were close to Sorrelle's Hickman line being removed. This line into her chest is no ordinary line – it's the line initially used to treat her cancer and, more lately, to administer her chemical feeds. Gem and Dean remember only too well the day when the Hickman line was first put into their daughter's chest and, more significantly, what it stood for. Numbness hits you when you realise why this line is needed and what is to follow. The line was fitted the day after her diagnosis in August 2015, and since then lines with infections have been removed and replaced. Five lines have been fitted for Sorrelle to receive chemotherapy and antibiotics. Throughout this journey we as a family have longed for the day this line would be removed for the last time, so we'd be able to hold her close without worrying about hurting her, have no more hospital stays, and feel genuine hope for this little girl. The day when the line would no longer be required because there's no cancer.

And so ... drum roll ... at approximately 5pm, Sorrelle went to theatre, where, for the final time, the Hickman line was removed! There will be no more chemical feeds, no more line infections and forced hospital stays – no more chemotherapy! We've taken the penultimate step to the end of treatment. The final step to remove the gastro tube will be pretty soon. Gemma and Dean released their little girl to the care of the surgeons safe in the knowledge that upon her return, life would not be quite the same. And so it was, that their daughter returned an hour later, and her loving parents were now able to consider what she might like to eat, knowing there would never again be a night where she's attached to wires and machines to feed her. This may be her final night on Ward 84 – the ward that has delivered so many emotions to this family and others. For Gemma and Dean, so many nights wondering what the future might bring, days swinging from despair to hope, frustration to determination, anxiety to relief. It was a journey into the unknown and, in a strange twist today, a journey into the unknown with a much brighter outlook.

The picture tonight of Sorrelle was taken about an hour after theatre. What better way to spend your 604th day after diagnosis than to tuck into a yummy Easter egg!

As I write this post, which will perhaps be one of a final few I pen, I feel we've reached that time when we can finally release the emotions we've kept locked away – the real worry you can't show, the devastation that hides in your mind, the sorrow that engulfs your heart. And when you know all will be well, those painful emotions can be replaced by a joy and a relief that is impossible to explain. We all hoped and dared to believe this day would come. And here we are, and in the middle of it all a slightly bigger small boat in a big ocean. She really is about to disembark and place her little feet on the shore!

I want to thank you, Gemma and Dean's army! If Sorrelle has in some way been an inspiration for you, then in return I can tell you that you have been her prayers. You have been Gemma's and Dean's strength. You have been the support we all needed to survive this. You helped save not just a special little girl but a very special family. I am truly humbled by the kindness and support you have shown throughout this journey. Thank you.

You have read this part so many times, but, as always, I shall update again in a week to report on the gastro tube and how the little munchkin is doing.

A very happy Easter to you all.

Grandpa

24th April 2017

Caption: What's out there, Daddy?

your future, Daughter ♡

A very good evening, everyone. So, you know our little hero has no Hickman line and everything since has been totally fine. She's been eating really well, and her calcium's been increased a little while her body learns how to retain it better.

Sorrelle had a truly magical time at Chester Zoo – her first visit as these trips were prohibited while the Hickman line was in. We are now left with the gastro tube. This has no purpose other than to give her medicine. Gemma has started to give this to Sorrelle orally and although a couple of them are not exactly tasty, Sorrelle is tolerating them. Because the line developed a blockage, it's been decided she should have it taken out. The last step is very close now!

I'll update again next week, but if I had to sum up this last week in one wonderful word, it would be 'normal'!

Catch you all next week.

Grandpa

29th April 2017

Caption: Zero to hero in four days (and a first spell on ICU)

Good evening, all, and welcome to the roller coaster that is Sorrelle's journey. Let me explain. The picture is from Wednesday, when sadly our little hero was admitted to hospital listless and with a temp of 39.8. It was clear she'd picked up a bad bug and become severely dehydrated. There were some concerns around her kidney function, and it wasn't until yesterday, after a host of antibiotics and lots of adjusted fluids, that things started to improve. This morning she was much more alert, but after I visited her earlier today, she became listless again. The conclusion is that she has a virus that's knocked her for six and will take her a few more days to get over. ICU did a great job in keeping her safe whilst the medicine did its job.

And so to the video. This was taken this evening and is evidence of two things – that Sorrelle will be OK, and that you now know what cute looks like! I tried to watch without smiling and failed miserably! Hopefully she will sleep well tonight, and then Grandpa will too! Until, of course, she wants breakfast!

So there you have this week's post. Certainly not what we expected and came as a bit of a shock, but hopefully by mid-week the little hero will be home.

Have a good weekend, all.

Grandpa

MAY 2017

7th May 2017

Caption: Arise, Sir Daddy!

A very good evening to you all and welcome to the latest update on Sorrelle and her progress. For the very first time throughout her journey, she was admitted to ICU, where we spent a rather worrying three days. We should, of course, have remembered that Sorrelle does insist on keeping us on our toes. This latest episode was no exception. Thankfully, she improved and was moved to her second home (Ward 84), where she spent a few more days.

I'm delighted to report she is once again well and back at home. You may notice she looks less chubby – this last episode took it out of her and she did lose a little weight. Since then, she's started to eat and begun to gain back the weight. There's no great concern and she's been pretty much grazing all day during a fun-packed day at Chester Zoo with her sister and one of her cousins. (There were, of course, a couple of adults around too!)

Today's picture was taken a few days ago, on her first visit to the beach. As you can see, it seemed to agree with her. As for all things medical, well, we await news on the removal of her gastro tube. Aside from that, nothing to report, other than a wonderful new normality! Let's hope there are no more nasty bugs, and Sorrelle is able to have a good long run of keeping well and getting bigger and stronger.

Will update again next week.

Take care, all.

Grandpa

17th May 2017

Caption: Skittles announce a new hero flavour!

A very good evening, everyone. About time for a Sorrelle update. This will be a pretty short one because our hero is both happy and well. There have been no medical issues at all, she's eating really well, gaining weight, and it's only a matter of time before the gastro tube will be removed. We should have some more information on that after Friday's review at the hospital. It is a joy to see her so happy.

Last weekend for the first time since before diagnosis she sat with Grandpa and ate some Weetabix ("bix" to Sorrelle). I cannot express how much I have missed this. And to have it start again is magical, knowing with every spoonful she is getting better and better. Her bowel is functioning not just normally following her stoma reversal, but it actually seems to be better than pre-diagnosis! Once again, a Sorrelle twist – but this time a wonderfully positive one.

I will update again on Sunday after her check-up but, for now, enjoy the picture and that cheeky smile and marvel at this small boat crossing that big ocean and about to step ashore!

Take care, all.

Grandpa

17th May 2017

A little extra. No caption, just sisters with a future together ♥♡

JUNE 2017

3rd June 2017

Caption: Hey, big sister. New house, big garden, new swing, and Mum and Dad paying for the lot. We're onto a winner here! 😊

A very good evening, everyone, and welcome to the latest update on Sorrelle. You will all be delighted to know that our little hero has had no medical mishaps and has remained at home. Today's caption picture is evidence of a very happy child, who has a new home to fill with wonderful times and new memories. Sorrelle's continuing to eat well, and Gemma has persisted with oral medication rather than depend on the gastro tube, which will eventually be removed – the last major medical procedure Sorrelle will have to give her a more normal life.

So, given I've just made mention of said gastro tube, it's only fair to share with you that we have a provisional date of 15th June for its removal. I am sure you will all share in our delight of this news, which marks the beginning of a new chapter for Sorrelle. As with the start of any new chapter, we will see an end to the previous one, much of which we'll be happy to see relegated to the past.

This will be an apt point to bring my updates to an end. Sorrelle's page will remain open for any future posts Gemma or Dean may wish to add, but it seems an appropriate time for Grandpa to step into the background.

I will update again in two weeks after Sorrelle's check-up and then post a final update following the gastro tube removal. For now, do enjoy those wonderful smiles on today's caption picture. And, as always, thank you for your continued love and support.

Grandpa

15th June 2017

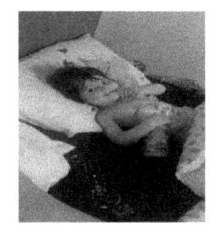

Caption: Day 664. 5am and ready.

Good morning, everyone, and welcome to a very brief update on Sorrelle. At 9:05am Sorrelle began her final journey to theatre, where she will have her gastro tube removed! The last visible sign of her two-year battle against cancer – and recognition that the battle is well and truly won! This brave little girl will finally begin to experience the normality we all take for granted. We long to hold her close without worrying if her little body pressing against us causes her any pain, about how she feels every time she looks at her tube, and having to be ever so careful that she doesn't catch it and get distressed. The procedure taking place right now will free her from all this and return her to the business of being a little girl.

I will post later to confirm all is well and then in a few days' time with my final post.

Take care, all.

Grandpa

15th June 2017

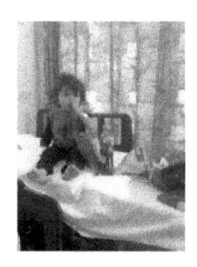

Caption: They call it post-op pretzels!

As promised, a very quick update. As you can see, Sorrelle is now back from theatre and, in typical fashion, taking everything in her stride. Her medicine? Why, pretzels, of course! The procedure went perfectly, and she'll be let out around lunchtime. We'll give her a few days to heal, and then I'll post my final Sorrelle update on Sunday.

Again, thank you for your love and support. I know Gem and Dean are very touched and grateful.

Have a good day, all.

Grandpa

17th June 2017

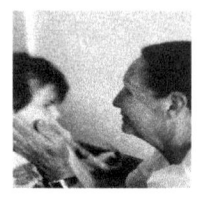

Caption: Hey little one you did it, I'm so proud of you

Had to mention Sorrelle's great grandma "De de". She watched her son watch his daughter watch her daughter! Mums delight that Sorrelle emerged victorious was etched in every pore. Relly loves you great grandma and thank you for being the warm supportive lady you have always been, couldn't have got through this without you.

19th June 2017

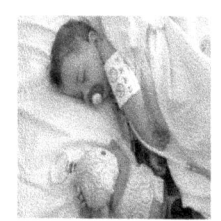

Caption: Then and now. Sleep and chocolate face. Kinda sums me up, Grandpa

Hello, everyone, and welcome to what will be my final update on Sorrelle. The many emotions I feel in writing this last post pale into insignificance when I think of how Gemma and Dean must feel. 667 days ago, they were given the news all parents dread but very few ever contemplate happening to them. On 21st August 2015, we were that family. The very next day, we began to realise that no family is immune from illness, disease and anguish. What we were later to discover is that what defines a family is how they deal with these unwelcome imposters. You see the bravery, courage, love, skill, care, support and determination on the face of every family member who visits. On the face of every medic, nurse, friend and workmate, and you marvel at the human spirit, never giving up despite the odds.

In the middle of this chaos, a ten-month-old baby who knows and understands nothing of what's going on. The cot in hospital is just geography. The hospital toys are still toys. The doctors and nurses are just more people to smile at, and Mummy and Daddy are still just that – Mummy and Daddy. This little face smiles at you, and you realise that she, and only she, will give you the courage to stay the course, face the battles and never give up on her. I can tell you that for every one of the 16,000 hours since diagnosis, Sorrelle gave us that. Her gift to us all bound us in a way even the closest family didn't think possible. It allowed us to understand each other more, it brought us closer together, it rallied us, and it helped shape our lives and priorities forever. A family in the midst of this needs support. And so to you – the army of readers, followers, friends, workmates and friends of friends – I would like to take a moment to thank you all. I have said so many times just how important you all are to Gemma and Dean and indeed our whole family. We will forever be in your debt.

One very important thing you realise is that, even with all this support at the centre, there needs to be a core of skilled doctors and nurses applying today's science with astounding care. For Professor Rob Wynn, the man responsible for saving Sorrelle – there are simply no words that can convey how we feel. For the nurses who cared for Sorrelle and supported us in the most extreme circumstances, who cried with us and laughed with us – again, no words come close. And to the lady in the South of England whose bone marrow not once but twice gave Sorrelle the gift of life – who will sadly never read this and understand the difference she made to a whole family – I think of her every single day, and I know Gemma and Dean do too.

There are other people we think of every day. People very dear to us. Those parents who had to face something far more painful than us. Those beautiful amazing children who were, and will always be, part of Sorrelle's life. Those angels at rest remind me every day of just how fortunate we are. Thank you, little ones, for the gift of your smiles, which will stay with us and your parents, whom we hold so dear.

Cancer does not care about your age, your race or your sex. It has been our biggest fear for generations and it still takes lives. What we know as a family is you can never give up. I truly hope that if, God forbid, this awful disease should strike, you'll reach this day, like us. You'll pace miles of hospital corridors, drink gallons of coffee, laugh when you want to cry, cry when you think there can't be tears left, eat awful food and hardly ever sleep, but life is worth it! And your child's smile will refuel you.

And so, after experiencing many dark days and nights, some of which we kept from you when Sorrelle's little life hung in the balance, we find ourselves almost a million minutes later in a truly wonderful place – Sorrelle has no wires, virtually no medication, and … drum roll … NO CANCER!

She did it! We did it! You did it!

Today, Sorrelle is so very well, eating, laughing, playing and just getting on with being a very determined and cheeky little girl (can't imagine where she gets it from!). She even has her name down to start nursery in September! Oh, and nothing medical to report!

As I approach the end, I would like to thank you all for giving me the great privilege of keeping you informed about this little munchkin. I thank you for putting up with the ramblings of an old grandpa and almost being my counsellors through this.

My final thanks go to Gemma and Dean for being truly great parents. I know we all like to think of ourselves as great parents and that we understand what other parents are going through, but I can't truly understand what Gem and Dean have been through. Gem and Dean, you are my inspiration and my benchmark for being a parent. The bravery and courage you have shown is astounding and humbling. Sorrelle, and now the gorgeous little Olivia, are so fortunate to have you as parents.

Today's caption pictures give you the start and end of this journey, or should I say *chapter*, for Sorrelle. The next chapter is just beginning, and it will be Gemma and Dean who bring you news of this. The Sorrelle posts will stay. It is simply Grandpa who's stepping back.

I've attached a video for you all, which quite rightly gives the last words to that little boat, who has very firmly docked at the shore.

Have a great day.

Grandpa

THE BEGINNING!